The Conditionality of Life

An Outline of the Twenty-Four Conditions as taught in the Abhidhamma

by *Nina van Gorkom*

ZOLAG
2010

First edition published in 2010 by
Zolag
32 Woodnook Road
Streatham
London
SW16 6TZ
www.zolag.co.uk

ISBN 978-1-897633-26-7

British Library Cataloguing in Publication Data
A CIP record for this book is available from the British Library
Printed in the UK and USA by Lightningsource.
$Id: cond.texi,v 1.34 2010/06/03 08:55:26 alan Exp alan $

Table of Contents

Preface ... 1

1 Introduction ... 5

2 Root-Condition ... 11

3 Object-Condition ... 19

4 Predominance-Condition ... 27

5 Proximity and Contiguity-Condition ... 35

6 Conascence and Mutuality-Condition ... 41

7 Dependence-Condition ... 47

8 Decisive Support-Condition (Part I) ... 51

9 Decisive Support-Condition (Part II) ... 57

10 Prenascence, Postnascence-Condition ... 65

11 Repetition-Condition ... 71

12 Kamma and Vipāka-Condition ... 77

13 Nutriment-Condition ... 85

14 Faculty-Condition ... 91

15 Jhāna-Condition ... 101

16 Path-Condition ... 109

17 Three Pairs of Conditions **117**

18 Aspects of the Twenty-Four Conditions **125**

Appendix 1 .... **131**

Appendix 2 .... **133**

Appendix 3 .... **135**

Glossary **137**

Books **143**

Books written by Nina van Gorkom 143

Books translated by Nina van Gorkom 143

Preface

The Buddha's teaching on the conditions for the phenomena of our life to arise has been laid down in the last of the seven books of the Abhidhamma, the "Paṭṭhāna", or "Conditional Relations". The Buddha, in the night he attained enlightenment, penetrated all the different conditions for the phenomena which arise and he contemplated the "Dependant Origination" (Paticca Samuppāda), the conditions for being in the cycle of birth and death, and the way leading to the elimination of these causes. We read in the Introduction of the "Atthasālinī" (The Expositor, the Commentary to the Dhammasangaṇi, the first book of the Abhidhamma) that the Buddha, during the fourth week after his enlightenment, sat in the "Jewel House", in the north west direction, and contemplated the Abhidhamma. The Abhidhamma was laid down later on in seven books. We read:

> . . . And while he contemplated the contents of the "Dhammasangaṇi", his body did not emit rays; and similarly with the contemplation of the next five books. But when, coming to the "Great Book", he began to contemplate the twenty-four universal causal relations of condition, of presentation, and so on, his omniscience certainly found its opportunity therein. For as the great fish Timirati-piṅgala finds room only in the great ocean eighty-four thousand yojanas in depth, so his omniscience truly finds room only in the Great Book. Rays of six colours-indigo, golden, red, white, tawny, and dazzling-issued from the Teacher's body, as he was contemplating the subtle and abstruse Dhamma by his omniscience which had found such opportunity . . .

The teaching of the conditional relations is deep and it is not easy to read the "Paṭṭhāna", but we could at least begin to study different conditions and verify them in daily life. Before we knew the Buddha's teachings we used to think of cause and effect in a speculative way. We may have reflected on the origin of life, on the origin of the world, we may have thought about causes and effects with regard to the events of life, but we did not penetrate the real conditions for the phenomena of life. The Buddha taught the way to develop understanding of what is true in the absolute or ultimate sense. We cannot understand the "Paṭṭhāna" if we do not know the difference between what is real in conventional sense and what is real in the ultimate sense. Body and mind are real in conventional sense, they are not real in the ultimate sense. What we call body and mind are temporary combinations of different realities which arise because of conditioning factors and then fall away immediately. They are succeeded by new realities which fall away again, and thus life goes on. Body, mind, person or being do not exist in the ultimate sense. Mental phenomena, nāma, and physical phenomena, rūpa, are real in the ultimate sense, but they are merely passing phenomena. Ultimate truth is not abstract. Ultimate realities, in Pāli: paramattha dhammas, have each their own characteristic which cannot be changed. We may change the name, but the characteristic remains the same. Seeing is an ultimate reality, it experiences visible object which appears through the eyes; it is real for everyone, it has its own unalterable characteristic. Anger has its own characteristic, it is real for everyone, no matter how we name it. Ultimate realities can be directly experienced when they appear through eyes, ears, nose, tongue, bodysense or mind. They arise because of their appropriate conditions.

There are twenty-four classes of conditions enumerated in the "Paṭṭhāna". In order to understand these it is essential to have a precise knowledge of the realities to which these conditional relations pertain. The "Dhammasangaṇi", the first book of the Abhidhamma, is an analytical exposition of all classes of consciousness, cittas, and their accompanying mental factors, cetasikas, and all physical phenomena, rūpas. The Dhammasangaṇi explains which cetasikas accompany which cittas[1]. It explains which rūpas arise together in a group and the factors which produce rūpas, namely, kamma, citta, nutrition and temperature. However, it does not describe in detail the different types of conditions. The Paṭṭhāna describes in detail all possible relations between phenomena. Each reality in our life can only occur because of a concurrence of different conditions which operate in a very intricate way. Hearing is conditioned by sound which impinges on the earsense. Both sound and earsense are rūpas which also arise because of their own conditions and fall away. Thus, hearing, the reality which they condition, cannot last either; it also has to fall away. Each conditioned reality can exist just for an extremely short moment. When we understand this it will be easier to see that there is no self who can exert control over realities. How could we control what falls away immediately? When we move our hands, when we walk, when we laugh or cry, when we are attached or worried, there are conditions for such moments. The Paṭṭhāna helps us to understand the deep underlying motives for our behaviour and the conditions for our defilements. It explains, for example, that kusala, wholesomeness, can be the object of akusala citta, unwholesome citta. For instance, on account of generosity which is wholesome, attachment, wrong view or conceit, which are unwholesome realities, can arise. The Paṭṭhāna also explains that akusala can be the object of kusala, for example, when akusala is considered with insight. This is an essential point which is often overlooked. If one thinks that akusala cannot be object of awareness and right understanding, the right Path cannot be developed.

The enumerations and classifications in the Paṭṭhāna may, at first sight, seem dry and cumbersome, but when they are carefully considered it can be seen that they deal with realities of daily life. The study of the Abhidhamma can become very lively and interesting if our knowledge is applied in our own situation. It can be understood more clearly that kusala citta and akusala citta arise because of different conditions. One may doubt whether it is helpful to know details about realities and their conditions. It is beneficial to have less ignorance about ourselves. Defilements cannot be eradicated immediately, there will still be sadness, worry and frustration. However, when it is more clearly understood that realities arise because of their own conditions there will be less inclination to try to do what is impossible: to change and to control what has arisen because of conditions. When there is more understanding one will be less obsessed by one's experiences, there will be more patience. The Paṭṭhāna clarifies how the arising of kusala and akusala at the present are conditions for the arising of kusala and akusala in the future.

[1] There is only one citta at a time but it is accompanied by several cetasikas which each perform their own function.

Each citta that arises and falls away is succeeded immediately by a following citta and therefore wholesome and unwholesome inclinations can be accumulated from moment to moment. Understanding that arises now falls away, but it is accumulated and thus, it can grow. It can develop to direct understanding of realities and it can eventually lead to enlightenment. The study of the Paṭṭhāna can encourage us to develop understanding together with all good qualities.

The reader will find it complicated to study the duration of rūpa which equals seventeen moments of citta. We could never count such moments, they pass too quickly. However, the knowledge about the duration of rūpa helps us to see that rūpa lasts longer than citta. Rūpa is weak at its arising moment, but after its arising it can condition citta. One rūpa can condition several cittas since it lasts longer than citta. For instance, the rūpa which is sense object (colour, sound, etc.) can condition a series of cittas arising in a sense-door process by way of object-condition, that is to say, by being the object they experience. The rūpas which are the sense-organs (eyesense, earsense, etc.) can condition citta by being its base, the place of origin. Thus, knowing about the duration of rūpa and of citta clarifies their relationship.

The Abhidhamma, the Suttanta and the Vinaya all point to the same goal: the eradication of wrong view and all other defilements. When we study the Paṭṭhāna we are reminded of this goal. Some people doubt whether the Buddha himself taught the twenty-four classes of conditions. They wonder why these have not been enumerated in the suttas. The nucleus of the teaching on conditions is to be found also in other parts of the teachings. In the suttas we read, for example, about jhāna-factors and Path-factors, and about the factors which are predominance-condition[2] for the realities they accompany, and these are among the twenty-four classes of conditions which are described in the Paṭṭhāna. The "Dependant Origination" (Paṭiccasamuppāda), the Buddha's teaching on the factors which are the conditions for being in the cycle of birth and death and also those which condition freedom from the cycle, is found in all parts of the scriptures. The teaching of the "Dependant Origination" is closely connected with the teaching of the "Paṭṭhāna", and the "Dependant Origination" cannot be understood without knowledge of the different types of conditions as taught in the "Paṭṭhāna". Doubt will only disappear if we thoroughly consider the different types of conditions, because then we can see for ourselves whether the contents of the "Paṭṭhāna" conform to the truth or not.

The twenty-four conditions have also been explained by the great commentator Buddhaghosa in the "Visuddhimagga" (Path of Purification[3]). Buddhaghosa, who lived in the beginning of the fifth century A.D. in Sri Lanka, edited older commentarial texts he found there.

I have used Pāli terms next to the English translation of these terms for precision. In different English textbooks one and the same Pāli term has been translated with different English words, and hence there may be confusion as to which reality is represented by such or such English word. Only part of the "Paṭṭhāna" has been translated into English by Ven. U Narada. This work, consisting of two volumes,

---

[2] Later on I shall deal with these kinds of conditions.

[3] I have used the translation by Ven. yāṇamoli, Colombo, 1964.

is, under the title of "Conditional Relations", available at the Pāli Text Society. The "Guide to Conditional Relations", which the translator also wrote, is a helpful introduction to the reading of the "Paṭṭhāna"[4]. All the texts from which I quoted are available at the Pāli Text Society. In Thailand, Ms. Sujin Boriharnwanaket is teaching and explaining the Dhamma in lectures, radio programs and meetings. In the Bovoranives Temple in Bangkok, she gave most inspiring lectures on the conditional relations. She stressed time and again that conditions pertain to this very moment, in daily life. I used many of her lively illustrations and her quotations from the scriptures for this book on conditions.

I have added an appendix where I explain some notions of the Abhidhamma in order to facilitate the reading of this study on conditions.

It has been said in commentaries that Buddhism will decline and that the Buddhist scriptures will disappear. The Abhidhamma, and in particular the "Paṭṭhāna", will be the first to be lost. The "Paṭṭhāna" is deep and difficult to understand. I hope I can contribute with this book to the arousing of interest in the "Paṭṭhāna". May the Abhidhamma survive for an additional length of time. This would also insure the survival of the other parts of the scriptures, the Vinaya and the Suttanta.

Theoretical knowledge of conditions is not the purpose of the "Paṭṭhāna". Conditions cannot be thoroughly grasped through mere intellectual understanding. The "Paṭṭhāna" helps us to have more understanding of the truth of non-self. It thereby encourages us to develop the eightfold Path, to develop direct understanding of all realities which appear through the five sense-doors and through the mind-door. When understanding of nāma, mental phenomena, and rūpa, physical phenomena, has been developed to the degree of the second stage of insight[5], the conditionality of realities will be directly understood. When conditions are understood more clearly, we shall be less inclined to cling to a self who could control awareness of nāma and rūpa. Thus, the "Paṭṭhāna" can help us to follow the right practice. It is above all the right practice of the eightfold Path that can promote the survival of the Buddha's teachings.

---

[4] See also "Guide to the Abhidhamma Piṭaka", Ch VII, by Ven. Nyanatiloka, B.P.S. Kandy, and "The Buddhist Philosophy of Relations", by Ven. Ledi Sayadaw, Department of Religious Affairs, Rangoon, Myanmar.

[5] Insight, direct understanding of nāma and rūpa, is developed in several stages, until realities are seen as they are at the attainment of enlightenment. The second stage cannot be realised before the first stage: knowing the difference between the characteristic of nāma and of rūpa.

1 Introduction

It is not by mere chance that we are born in planes of existence where we can experience objects through the senses and that we are equipped with sense-organs through which we can experience such objects. During previous lives as well we experienced colour, sound and other sense-objects. We were clinging to these objects in the past and we are clinging to them at present again and again, so that attachment has become a deeprooted tendency. Attachment does not arise with each moment of consciousness, citta, but the tendency to attachment is "carried on" from one moment to the next moment, from life to life. Each citta which arises falls away completely, but it is succeeded by the next citta. In the uninterrupted series of cittas which are succeeding one another continuously, inclinations to both good and evil are carried on.

We all have accumulated attachment. For instance, as soon as a morsel of delicious food is on our tongue, attachment to flavour has an opportunity to arise. In the human plane of existence there are many opportunities for attachment to sense-objects. There were wise people, also before the Buddha's time, who saw the disadvantage of the experience of sense-objects. They cultivated tranquil meditation to the stage of absorption, jhāna, in order to temporarily suppress the clinging to sense-objects. Jhānacittas of the different stages of jhāna can produce results in the form of rebirth in higher planes of existence where there are less sense impressions or none at all. In these planes one does not have to take food in order to stay alive, there are no conditions for the enjoyment of flavours. Through the cultivation of jhāna, however, clinging is not eradicated. So long as clinging has not been eradicated rebirth will occur. When the lifespan in a higher plane is terminated one may be reborn in a plane where one will cling again to sense-objects and accumulate more clinging, unless one develops the wisdom which can eradicate clinging.

The fact that we are born in the human plane where we can enjoy flavours and all the other sense-objects and also the fact that we have clinging to them is conditioned. When we use the word "condition" we should realize that there is not just one kind of condition which brings about one kind of effect. There are many types of conditions for the phenomena which arise and it is important to study these different types. We may be inclined to put off the study of this subject because we think it too difficult. However, we should remember that conditions are real in daily life and that they are not merely textbook terms.

We may have learnt that there are different types of mental phenomena, nāmas, and different types of physical phenomena, rūpas, and that these are only conditioned phenomena. If we study the conditions for the arising of nāma and rūpa we shall have more understanding of the meaning of "no self". The study of the teachings and consideration of what one has learnt are important conditions for the arising of sati, awareness, and direct understanding of realities and this will eventually lead to the eradication of the wrong view of self.

Awareness or mindfulness, sati, is a sobhana cetasika, beautiful mental factor, which arises with each wholesome citta. Sati is non-forgetful of what is wholesome, and there are many levels of sati. Sati in the development of insight, vipassanā, is directly aware of the nāma or rūpa which appears.

What we take for our life is actually conditioned phenomena (saṅkhāra dhammas), that is, citta (consciousness), cetasikas (mental factors accompanying citta), and rūpa (physical phenomena). What arises because of conditions does not last, it has to fall away again. Thus, citta, cetasika and rūpa are impermanent. Nibbāna is the unconditioned dhamma, it does not arise and it does not fall away.

Citta experiences something, it cognizes an object. The five senses and the mind are the doorways through which citta can cognize the different objects which present themselves. Citta does not arise singly, it is always accompanied by cetasikas. Cetasikas have each their own function and assist citta in cognizing an object. There are many ways of classifying cittas and one of these is by way of four "jātis" or classes (jāti literally means birth or nature). There are four jātis by which the different nature of cittas is shown and they are:

- kusala (wholesome)
- akusala (unwholesome)
- vipāka (result which may be pleasant or unpleasant)
- kiriya (neither cause nor result, inoperative)

Cetasikas are of the same jāti as the citta they accompany. There are seven cetasikas, the "universals" (sabba-citta-sādhārana) which accompany every citta[1]. There are six cetasikas, the "particulars" (pakiṇṇakā) which arise with cittas of the four jātis but not with every citta[2]. Furthermore, there are akusala cetasikas which arise only with akusala cittas and there are sobhana (beautiful) cetasikas which arise only with sobhana cittas. Citta and the accompanying cetasikas, in the planes of existence where there are nāma and rūpa, arise at the same physical base (vatthu)[3], they experience the same object and they fall away together. Citta and cetasikas are of the same plane of consciousness[4]: they can be of the sense-sphere, they can be jhānacitta which is rūpāvacara or arūpāvacara, or they can be lokuttara (supramundane), experiencing nibbāna. Citta and cetasikas condition one another in several ways, as we shall see.

Rūpas, physical phenomena, do not arise singly, but in groups, which can be produced by kamma, by citta, by heat or by nutrition[5]. Thus we see that there is no reality which arises singly. Realities do not arise by their own power, they are

---

[1] They are contact, feeling, remembrance or perception (saññā), volition, concentration, life faculty and attention.

[2] They are: initial thinking, sustained thinking, decision, effort, rapture and wish-to-do.

[3] In the planes of existence where there are nāma and rūpa, cittas do not arise independently of the body, they have a physical base or place of origin, vatthu, which is rūpa. For example, the rūpa which is eyesense is the base for seeing-consciousness, and the other senses are the bases for the relevant sense-cognitions.

[4] Plane of existence refers to the place where one is born, such as the human plane, a hell plane or a heavenly plane. Plane of consciousness refers to the nature of citta, namely cittas of the sense sphere which experience sense objects, jhānacittas which experience with absorption meditation subjects or lokuttara cittas which experience nibbāna, the unconditioned dhamma.

[5] Different groups of rūpas of the body are produced by one these four factors, and rūpas which are not of the body are produced only by temperature.

dependant on other phenomena which make them arise. Moreover, no reality arises from a single cause, there is a concurrence of several conditions for realities to arise. When we, for example, taste delicious cheese, there are several conditions for tasting-consciousness. Tasting-consciousness is vipākacitta, result, produced by kamma. It is also conditioned by the rūpa which is tastingsense, produced by kamma as well. Tastingsense is the physical place of origin or base (vatthu) for tasting-consciousness as well as the doorway (dvara) through which tasting-consciousness experiences the flavour. The rūpa which is flavour is a condition for tasting-consciousness by being its object. Contact, phassa, which is a cetasika accompanying every citta, "contacts" the flavour so that tasting-consciousness can experience it. Without phassa citta could not experience any object.

If we understand that each reality depends on a multiplicity of conditions we shall be less inclined to think that pain and pleasure can be controlled by a self. There are many moments of pleasure and pain, each brought about by their own conditions. When we study the conditions for the phenomena which arise, we shall better understand that there is no self which has any power over them.

Nāma conditions rūpa and rūpa conditions nāma. We read in the "Visuddhimagga" (XVIII, 32) about the interdependence of nāma and rūpa:

> "...For just as when two sheaves of reeds are propped up one against the other, each one gives the other consolidating support, and when one falls the other falls, so too, in the five-constituent becoming (in the plane of the five khandhas[6]), mentality-materiality occurs as an interdependent state, each of its components giving the other consolidating support, and when one falls owing to death, the other falls too. Hence the Ancients said:
>
> The mental and material
> Are twins and each supports the other;
> When one breaks up they both break up
> Through interconditionality.
>
> And just as when sound occurs having as its support a drum that is beaten by the stick, then the drum is one and the sound is another, the drum and the sound are not mixed up together, the drum is void of the sound and the sound is void of the drum, so too, when mentality occurs having as its support the materiality called the physical base, the door and the object, then the materiality is one and the mentality is another, the mentality and the materiality are not mixed up together, the mentality is void of the materiality and the materiality is void of the mentality; yet the mentality occurs due to the materiality as the sound occurs due to the drum..."

---

[6] The conditioned phenomena of our life can be classified as five khandhas or aggregates: rūpa-kkhandha, vedanā-kkhandha (feeling), saññā-kkhandha (perception or remembrance), saṅkhāra-kkhandha (formations, all cetasikas except feeling and perception), and viññāṇa-kkhandha (consciousness).

In being mindful of nāma and rūpa we shall learn to distinguish their different characteristics, thus, we shall not confuse nāma and rūpa and know them as conditioned realities, not self. The "Visuddhimagga" (XVII, 68) defines condition, paccaya, as follows:

> "... When a state is indispensable to another state's presence or arising, the former is a condition for the latter. But as to characteristic, a condition has the characteristic of assisting; for any given state that assists the presence or arising of a given state is called the latter's condition. The words, condition, cause, reason, source, originator, producer, etc., are one in meaning though different in letter..."

Thus, there are conditioning phenomena, paccaya-dhammas, and conditioned phenomena, paccayupanna-dhammas.

In the "Paṭṭhāna" there is a tripartite division of realities, which can also be found elsewhere in the Abhidhamma. Realities can be: kusala (here translated as faultless), akusala (faulty) and avyākatā (indeterminate), which comprises citta and cetasikas which are vipāka, kiriyacittas, rūpa and nibbāna.

The "Paṭṭhāna" deals with twenty-four classes of conditions and explains in detail the phenomena which condition other phenomena by way of these different conditions. One may wonder whether so many details are neces- sary.

We read in "The Guide"[7] (Netti-Pakaraṇaṁ, Part III, 16 Modes of Conveying, VII, Knowledge of the Disposition of Creatures' Faculties, paragraph 587):

> "Herein, the Blessed One advises one of keen faculties with advice in brief; the Blessed One advises one of medium faculties with advice in brief and detail; the Blessed One advises one of blunt faculties with advice in detail."

The Buddha taught Dhamma in detail to those who could not grasp the truth quickly. People today are different from people at the Buddha's time who could attain enlightenment quickly, even during a discourse. The "Paṭṭhāna" is not theory, it teaches the truth of conditioned phenomena in our own life and this can be verified. If we merely learn the theory of the different conditions we shall have the wrong grasp of the Abhidhamma and this leads to mental derangement, to madness. We read in the "Expositor"(I, Introductory Discourse, 24):

> "...The bhikkhu, who is ill trained in the Abhidhamma, makes his mind run to excess in metaphysical abstractions and thinks of the unthinkable. Consequently he gets mental distraction..."

We should keep in mind the purpose of the study of the conditions as taught in the "Paṭṭhāna." Each section illustrates the truth that what we take for self are only conditioned phenomena. We keep on forgetting the truth and thus we have to be reminded again and again.

We read in the "Visuddhimagga" (XX, 19) that the five khandhas (conditioned nāmas and rūpas) are "as a disease, because of having to be maintained by con-

---

[7] An ancient guide for commentators, from which also Buddhaghosa quoted. It is assumed that it came from India to Sri Lanka, between the 3rd century B.C. and the 5th century A.C.

ditions, and because of being the root of disease". The khandhas arise because of conditions and what arises because of a concurrence of conditions is not eternal, it has to fall away. Therefore, the khandhas cannot be a real refuge, they are dukkha, unsatisfactory. Further on we read that they are a calamity, an affliction, a plague, no protection, no shelter, as murderous, because of breaking faith like an enemy posing as a friend.

We cling to the khandhas, we want them to arise again and again; we wish life to continue. So long as we have not eradicated defilements, the khan- dhas will continue to arise at birth. We perform kamma, good or evil deeds, that can produce result in the form of future rebirth. We still run the risk of an unhappy rebirth produced by akusala kamma[8]. Kamma is accumulated and thus it is capable of producing result later on. Not only kamma, but also defilements are accumulated. Since there are many more akusala cittas arising than kusala cittas, we accumulate defilements again and again, and these cause sorrow. Akusala cittas which arose in the past condition the arising of akusala cittas later on, at present and in the future. The latent tendencies of akusala are like microbes infesting the body and they can become active at any time when the conditions are favorable. So long as the khandhas have not been fully understood by insight defilements have soil to grow in; they are not abandoned and thus the cycle of birth and death continues. In order eventually fully to understand the khandhas we should learn what the conditions are for the phenomena which arise. Therefore, it is beneficial to study the twenty-four conditions which are treated in the "Paṭṭhāna".

[8] Those who have attained one of the stages of enlightenment, the ariyans, have no conditions for an unhappy rebirth.

2 Root-Condition

The first condition mentioned in the "Paṭṭhāna" is root-condition, hetu-paccaya. There are three akusala hetus: lobha, attachment, dosa, aversion, and moha, ignorance, and these can have many degrees. Lobha can be a slight attachment or it can be clinging, greed or covetousness. Dosa can be a slight aversion, or it can be as intense as anger or hatred. Moha is ignorance of realities, it is ignorance of what is kusala or akusala, and ignorance of the four noble truths[1]. Moha is the root of all that is akusala, it arises with each akusala citta. There are three sobhana (beautiful) hetus: alobha, non-attachment or generosity, adosa, non-aversion or kindness, and amoha, paññā or right understanding. The three sobhana hetus can have many degrees, they can even be lokuttara (supramundane), when they accompany lokuttara citta which experiences nibbāna.

These six roots are actually cetasikas or mental factors which accompany citta. They are called root, since they are the firm foundation of the citta. Just as a tree rests on its roots and receives sap through the roots in order to grow, evenso are the akusala cittas and sobhana cittas dependent on the presence of the roots and they cannot occur in their absence. Thus, the roots are powerful conditions for the cittas which are rooted in them.

When akusala citta arises it is always rooted in moha, and it may have in addition the root of lobha or of dosa. The twelve types of akusala citta are classified according to hetu:

- eight types are rooted in moha and lobha, and they are called lobha-mūla-cittas[2],
- two types are rooted in moha and dosa, and they are called dosa-mūla-cittas[3],
- two types are rooted only in moha, and they are called moha-mūla-cittas[4].

All cittas accompanied by sobhana hetus are called sobhana cittas. Not only kusala citta, but also vipākacitta and kiriyacitta that are accompanied by sobhana hetus are sobhana cittas.

All sobhana cittas have to be rooted in alobha and adosa and they may or may not be rooted in amoha or paññā as well. There are eight types of mahā-kusala cittas (kusala cittas of the sense-sphere[5]), eight types of mahā-vipākacittas and

[1] The truth of dukkha, suffering, of the origin of dukkha, which is clinging, of the cessation of dukkha, which is nibbāna, and of the Path leading to the cessation of dukkha.

[2] Mūla also means root. Four types are accompanied by somanassa, pleasant feeling, four types by wrong view, four types are asaṅkhārika, not-induced or spontaneous, four types are sasaṅkhārika, induced. Altogether there are eight types.

[3] One type is not-induced and one type is induced.

[4] One is called accompanied by restlessness, uddhacca, and one is accompanied by doubt, vicikicchā.

[5] Mahā means great.

eight types of mahā-kiriyacittas (of the arahat[6]). Of each of the three sets of eight types, four types are accompanied by paññā and four types are not accompanied by paññā, thus, accompanied by the two sobhana hetus of alobha and adosa[7]. The sobhana hetus that accompany these sobhana cittas condition them by way of root-condition, hetu-paccaya.

People who develop samatha, tranquil meditation, may have accumulated skill for the attainment of jhāna, absorption. When there are the right conditions jhānacittas arise. There are jhānacittas of different stages of rūpa-jhāna, material jhāna, and arūpa-jhāna, immaterial jhāna[8]. The rūpa-jhānacittas (rūpāvacara cittas) and the arūpa-jhānacittas (arūpāvacara cittas) always have the three hetus of alobha, adosa and paññā, because absorption is not possible without paññā.

Through the development of insight, vipassanā, right understanding of realities gradually grows and when understanding has been developed to the degree that enlightenment can be attained, lokuttara cittas which experience nibbāna arise. Lokuttara cittas always have three hetus, they are accompanied by alobha (non-attachment), adosa (non-aversion) and paññā; these hetus are also lokuttara.

Not all cittas have hetus, there are also rootless cittas, ahetuka cittas which may be vipākacittas (result) or kiriyacittas (neither cause nor result, inoperative). When visible object impinges on the eyesense, it is experienced by cittas arising in the eye-door process[9]; it is experienced by seeing which is ahetuka vipākacitta, and by other ahetuka cittas and subsequently by cittas performing the function of javana (impulsion or "running through the object") arise, and these are (in the case of non-arahats) kusala cittas or akusala cittas and thus, with hetus. After the eye-door process is over, visible object is experienced through the mind-door; there is the mind-door adverting-consciousness which is ahetuka kiriyacitta, to be followed by javana-cittas which are kusala cittas or akusala cittas.

Good deeds or bad deeds are performed during the moments of javana. Then kamma is accumulated which can produce its result later on. One also accumulates good and bad inclinations which condition the arising of kusala citta or akusala citta in the future. When kusala javana-cittas are accompanied by paññā which is right understanding of realities, right understanding is accumulated.

---

6 The arahat does not have akusala cittas nor kusala cittas, he does not perform kamma which produces result. When he has sobhana cittas, cittas accompanied by beautiful qualities, they are inoperative, mahā-kiriyacittas which do not produce result.

7 Of each of the three sets of eight types, four types are associated with paññā, four types are without paññā, four types are accompanied by somanassa, pleasant feeling, four types are accompanied by upekkhā, indifferent feeling. Four types are asaṅkhārika, not induced, four types are sasaṅkhārika, induced.

8 The meditation subjects of rūpa-jhāna are dependant on materiality, whereas those of arūpa-jhāna do not and thus, arūpa-jhāna is more tranquil, more refined.

9 The objects which impinge on the six doors are experienced by several cittas arising in a process, which each perform their own function. Some of these cittas are ahetuka kiriyacitta, some ahetuka vipākacitta, and some are accompanied by roots, namely the javana-cittas which are either kusala cittas or akusala cittas. See Appendix 1.

As we have seen in the classification of cittas rooted in sobhana hetus, there are vipākacittas with hetus[10]. Kamma produces rebirth-consciousness, paṭisandhi-citta, which is vipākacitta, and this vipākacitta, depending on the type and degree of kamma which produces it, may be: ahetuka, or accompanied by two roots, namely alobha and adosa, or accompanied by three roots, that is to say, by paññā as well. The roots condition the citta and the accompanying cetasikas by way of root-condition. All bhavanga-cittas (life-continuum[11]) and the cuti-citta (dying-consciousness) are of the same type of vipākacitta as the paṭisandhi-citta.

It is important to know which type of citta arises at the present moment. Is it with roots or is it rootless? Is it akusala citta or kusala citta? Cittas rooted in lobha are bound to arise time and again, since lobha has been accumulated for aeons. The first javana-cittas of every living being are lobha-mūla-cittas; clinging is deeply rooted. One clings to all kinds of objects which present themselves through the six doors and clinging is extremely hard to eradicate. We read in the "Gradual Sayings" (Book of the Twos, Ch XI, paragraph1):

"Monks, there are these two longings hard to abandon. What two?

The longing for gain and the longing for life. These are the two."

Time and again we want to gain something for ourselves. When we get up in the morning and we eat breakfast we are clinging to coffee or tea, but we do not notice that there are the hetus of moha and lobha which condition the citta by way of root-condition. We cling to seeing or to visible object, but we do not notice it, we are so used to clinging. We have longing for life, we want to go on living and experiencing sense objects. That is why there are conditions for rebirth again and again. It is impossible for us not to have longing for life, only the arahat has eradicated it.

We would like to have kusala citta more often, but it cannot arise without the hetus which are alobha and adosa. Without these hetus we cannot perform any wholesome deed, we cannot speak with kindness and generosity. When amoha or paññā does not accompany the kusala citta, right understanding of realities cannot be developed. There is no self who can control hetu-paccaya, root-condition; akusala hetus and sobhana hetus are anattā.

The roots, hetus, are the dhammas which condition the citta and cetasikas they accompany and also the rūpa which is produced by the citta at that moment. For instance, lobha-mūla-citta, citta rooted in attachment, has two hetus: lobha, attachment, and moha, ignorance. Lobha and moha condition the citta and its accompanying cetasikas by way of root-condition. Moreover, rūpa produced by lobha-mūla-citta is also conditioned by the roots of lobha and moha. In the case of root-condition, the hetus which are the conditioning factors (the paccayas) and the dhammas they condition (the paccayupanna dhammas) arise simultaneously.

---

[10] Some vipākacittas are ahetuka, rootless, such as seeing-consciousness or hearing-consciousness, and some vipākacittas are accompanied by roots.

[11] Bhavanga-cittas arise in between the processes of cittas, they preserve the continuity in the life of a being. They do not experience the objects which impinge on the senses and the mind, they experience their own object, which is the same as the object experienced by the rebirth-consciousness. See my "Abhidhamma in Daily Life", Ch 12.

The "Paṭṭhāna" (Analytical Exposition, II, 1) gives the following definition of root-condition:

> "The roots are related to the states[12] which are associated with roots, and the rūpa produced thereby, by root-condition."

Citta is one of the four factors which can produce rūpas, the others being kamma, temperature (utu) and nutrition (āhāra). Citta can produce the groups of rūpa consisting of the eight inseparable rūpas which are: solidity, cohesion, temperature, motion, colour, odour, flavour and nutritive essence[13].

Citta produces the two kinds of intimation, namely: bodily intimation (kāya-viññatti), gestures, movements of the body and facial movements by which we express our intentions, and speech intimation (vacī-viññatti). Citta is assisted by the accompanying cetasikas when it produces rūpa.

When we are angry and we show this by our facial expression, akusala citta produces the rūpa which is bodily intimation, conditioned by the hetus which are moha and dosa by way of root-condition. We may raise our hand and hit someone else. Then akusala kamma through the body is being performed and the rūpas are conditioned by root-condition. When we flatter someone else in order to be liked by him we speak with lobha-mūla-citta. Then the rūpa which is speech-intimation is conditioned by moha and lobha by way of root-condition. Or we may commit akusala kamma through speech, for example, when we are lying. Lying may be done with lobha-mūla-citta when we want to gain something, or with dosa-mūla-citta when we want to harm someone else. The rūpa which is speech intimation is then conditioned by the accompanying roots by way of root-condition.

When we clean the house or when we cook, do we realize by which hetus our bodily movements are conditioned? There can be awareness at such moments. We may write a letter to someone else with kindness, mettā, and then the rūpas which arise while we move our hands are produced by kusala citta. The accompanying sobhana hetus condition these rūpas by way of root-condition. However, there are likely to be akusala cittas arising alternately with kusala cittas. There may be right understanding of nāma and rūpa while we write and then the citta is accompanied by alobha, adosa and amoha.

The rebirth-consciousness is vipākacitta, the result of kamma, a deed committed in the past. The rebirth-consciousness may be ahetuka (rootless) and in that case one is born handicapped[14]. Or the paṭisandhi-citta may be accompanied by two or three sobhana hetus, depending on the degree of kusala kamma which produces it. These hetus are of different degrees. When the paṭisandhi-citta is rooted in

---

12 "States"stands for dhammas, realities; "states which are associated with roots" are the realities which arise together with the roots, namely, citta and cetasikas.

13 Rūpas arise and fall away in groups or units, and these consist of at least eight rūpas, which are called the inseparable rūpas. Some groups of rūpas consist of more than eight rūpas, but the eight inseparables always have to be present.

14 The kusala kamma which produces a paṭisandhi-citta which is kusala vipāka without roots is weaker than the kusala kamma which produces a paṭisandhi-citta with two roots or three roots. There are many different kammas with different degrees which produce their results accordingly.

sobhana hetus, these hetus condition the citta, the accompanying cetasikas and the rūpas which are produced by kamma and which arise at the same time as the paṭisandhi-citta.

The paṭisandhi-citta cannot produce rūpa, but, in the planes where there are nāma and rūpa, the five khandha planes, the rūpas arising at the moment of birth are produced by kamma. Thus, both the paṭisandhi-citta and the rūpas which arise at the same moment are result of kamma, a deed previously done. In the case of human beings, kamma produces at the first moment of life three groups of rūpa, one group with the heartbase[15], one group with sex (male or female) and one group with bodysense. Since the kusala kamma which produces nāma and rūpa at the moment of birth can be of different degrees, the mental result and the bodily result it produces can also be of different degrees. We can see that human beings are born with different mental and bodily capacities. Some people are beautiful, some ugly, some are apt to few illnesses, some to many illnesses. When one is born with paññā, there are conditions to develop it during one's life, even to the degree of enlightenment. Thus we see that the diversity of the nāma and rūpa of human beings from the moment of birth is dependent on conditions.

The "Paṭṭhāna" (Faultless Triplet, kusala ttika, Ch VII, Investigation Chapter, Pañha-vāra, I, Conditions Positive, 1, Classification Chapter, Root 7, 403) states about root-condition at the first moment of life:

> "At the moment of conception, resultant indeterminate roots (hetus which are vipāka[16]) are related to (their) associated aggregates (khandhas)[17] and kamma-produced matter by root-condition."

Not only cittas of the sense-sphere, kāmāvacara cittas, which are accompanied by roots, are conditioned by these roots by way of root-condition, hetu-paccaya, also cittas of higher planes of consciousness, namely jhāna-cittas and lokuttara cittas, are conditioned by the accompanying roots by way of hetu-paccaya. As to rūpāvacara cittas (rūpa-jhānacittas), rūpāvacara kusala citta, rūpāvacara vipākacitta and rūpāvacara kiriyacitta (of the arahat) produce rūpas of the body. These rūpas are then conditioned by the hetus accompanying the rūpa-jhānacittas by way of hetu-paccaya. As to arūpāvacara cittas (arūpa-jhānacittas), arūpāvacara kusala citta and arūpāvacara kiriyacitta produce rūpas of the body, and these rūpas are then conditioned by the hetus accompanying those cittas by way of hetu-paccaya. Arūpāvacara vipākacittas do not produce any rūpa; these cittas which are the result of arūpa-jhāna, arise in arūpa-brahma planes where there is no rūpa,

---

15 In the planes of existence where there are nāma and rūpa citta must have a physical base or place of origin. For seeing, hearing and the other sense-cognitions the corresponding senses are the physical bases. All the other types of citta also have a physical base, and this rūpa is called the "heart-base".

16 As I explained in my Introduction, realities, dhammas, can be classified as threefold: as kusala, as akusala and as indeterminate, avyākatā. Indeterminate dhammas include vipāka and kiriya, inoperative. Thus, hetus which are "resultant indeterminate" are hetus which are vipāka.

17 The associated aggregates are the citta and cetasikas, which arise together with the roots.

only nāma[18]. Lokuttara cittas produce rūpas of the body[19]. The rūpa is then conditioned by hetus which are lokuttara, by way of hetu-paccaya.

In the "Paṭṭhāna" we read about many aspects of conditional relations between phenomena and we should consider these in our daily life. The study of root-condition can remind us to consider whether kusala citta or akusala citta arises while we act, speak or think.

The roots which arise together condition one another by way of root-condition. Alobha and adosa always arise together and they may or may not be accompanied by amoha, paññā. When there is amoha, the two other roots which accompany the citta, namely alobha and adosa, are conditioned by amoha. For instance, right understanding may accompany generosity, alobha. While we give we may realize that generosity is only a type of nāma, not self, and then the generosity is purer, it has a higher degree of wholesomeness than generosity which is not accompanied by right understanding. When someone is born with mahā-vipākacitta (vipākacitta of the sense-sphere accompanied by sobhana hetus), this citta may be accompanied by paññā or unaccompanied by paññā. When the paṭisandhi-citta is accompanied by paññā one may, if paññā is developed during that life, attain enlightenment.

Moha and lobha condition one another, and moha and dosa condition one another. We may find it difficult to know the characteristic of moha and we tend to forget that when there is lobha there is moha as well, or when there is dosa there is moha as well. We should remember that whenever akusala citta arises, there is ignorance of realities. When we, for example, cling to a pleasant sound, we are at such a moment blinded, we do not see the object as it really is, as a conditioned reality which is impermanent. When we are annoyed, there is dosa as well as ignorance. We do not like to have dosa because we do not like unpleasant feeling, but we do not understand the conditions for dosa, we forget that ignorance conditions it. When ignorance arises, we do not see the danger and disadvantage of akusala. When we develop mettā, dosa can be temporarily subdued, but for the eradication of dosa the development of right understanding of realities is necessary. Only the ariyan who has attained the third stage of enlightenment, the anāgāmī (non-returner), has developed paññā to such degree that dosa has been eradicated. Ignorance leads to all kinds of defilements and only right understanding of nāma and rūpa can finally eradicate ignorance.

The akusala hetus, unwholesome roots, are dangerous; they are accumulated and they cause the arising of akusala cittas again and again. They prevent us from kusala and cause disturbance of mind. We read in the "Itivuttaka" (Khuddhaka Nikāya, "As it was said", Book of the Threes, Ch IV, paragraph 9[20]) :

---

[18] The rebirth-consciousness in a higher plane of existence, namely, in a rūpa-brahma plane or an arūpa-brahma plane, is the result of jhāna.

[19] In the planes of existence where there are nāma and rūpa, citta produces rūpas such as solidity, heat, suppleness, etc. throughout life. The lokuttara citta which experiences nibbāna also produces such rūpas of the body.

[20] I am using the translation by Ven. Nyanaponika, in "Roots of Good and Evil", Wheel no. 251/ 253, B.P.S. Kandy.

"There are three inner taints, three inner foes, three inner enemies, three inner murderers, three inner antagonists. What are these three? Greed is an inner taint... Hatred is an inner taint... Delusion is an inner taint, an inner foe, an inner enemy, an inner murderer, an inner antagonist.

Greed is a cause of harm,
Unrest of mind it brings.
This danger that has grown within,
Blind folk are unaware of it.

A greedy person cannot see the facts
Nor can he understand the Dhamma.
When greed has overpowered him,
In complete darkness is he plunged.

But he who can forsake this greed
And what to greed incites, not craves,
From him will quickly greed glide off,
As water from the lotus leaf.

The sutta then speaks about the danger and the forsaking of hate and of delusion. We read about the forsaking of delusion:

But who has shed delusion's veil,
Is undeluded where confusion reigns,
He scatters all delusion sure,
Just as the sun dispels the night."

Feelings are also conditioned by the accompanying hetus by way of hetu-paccaya. Pleasant feeling is different depending on whether it accompanies akusala citta or kusala citta. There is unrest of mind with the pleasant feeling accompanying clinging and there is calm with the pleasant feeling accompanying generosity. When there is awareness, we may realize that these two kinds of pleasant feeling are different. It is useful to read about the different conditions for phenomena to arise; we should consider their implications in daily life, so that we can understand what kind of life we are leading. Is it a life full of lobha, dosa and moha, or is right understanding being developed?

3 Object-Condition

Each citta which arises experiences an object and the accompanying cetasikas also experience that object. The object conditions citta and the accompanying cetasikas because they experience that object. Thus, the object is in this case the conditioning factor, paccaya dhamma, and the citta and cetasikas are the conditioned realities, paccayupanna dhammas. Rūpa is not conditioned by way of object since rūpa does not experience any object.

We read in the "Paṭṭhāna" (Analytical Exposition of Conditions, 2):

> "Visible object-base is related to eye-consciousness element and its associated states by object-condition."

Visible object is also related to the other cittas of the eye-door process by way of object-condition. It is the same with sound and the other objects which can be experienced through the sense-doors and through the mind-door. They are related to the cittas concerned by way of object-condition.

Everything can be an object of experience. All conditioned nāmas and rūpas, present, past or future, the unconditioned dhamma which is nibbāna and also concepts which are not real in the ultimate sense can be object. Rūpa can be experienced through sense-door and through mind-door; citta, cetasika, nibbāna and concepts can be experienced only through mind-door. Visible object which is experienced by seeing has to arise before seeing arises and when seeing experiences it, it has not fallen away yet, since rūpa lasts as long as seventeen moments of citta[1].When visible object is experienced through the mind-door it has just fallen away. Also seeing can be object. Citta can, through the mind-door, experience another citta such as seeing which has just fallen away. It must have fallen away since only one citta at a time can arise. There may be, for example, a citta with understanding (paññā) which realizes seeing as a conditioned nāma which is impermanent.

For an object to be experienced, there must be contact, phassa. Phassa is a cetasika arising together with each citta and it "contacts" the object so that citta can cognize it. Contact is nāma, it is different from what we mean in conventional language by physical contact. There is contact through the eyes, the ears, the nose, the tongue, the bodysense and the mind. Phassa is an essential condition for citta to experience an object. The rūpa which is colour can only be object when phassa contacts it. It is the same with sound and the other objects.

What kind of objects does phassa contact? In order to have more understanding of the reasons why we have to experience particular objects we should consider the object-condition and other conditions. We may be in the company of a good friend in Dhamma so that we can hear the right Dhamma and are able to develop right understanding. Or we may be in the company of bad friends who are negligent of

---

[1] A sense-door process of cittas is followed by a mind-door process of cittas which experience the same sense object as the preceding sense-door process, but, since rūpa cannot last longer than seventeen moments of citta, that sense object has just fallen away when it is experienced by the cittas of the mind-door process which follows upon the sense-door process. Later on other mind-door processes of cittas can arise which experience concepts. See Appendix 1 and my "Abhidhamma in Daily Life", Ch 15.

what is wholesome. In these different situations it is phassa which contacts different objects. We may be inclined to think that we can choose the objects we experience. Even when it seems that we can choose, the experience of objects is still conditioned. When the conditions are not right, we cannot experience a particular object we wish to experience. For example, we may long for the flavour of apple and we start to eat it, but the inside may be spoilt and instead of a delicious flavour we taste a bitter flavour. Or we turn on the radio in order to hear music, but then we cannot hear it because the radio is out of order or the noise outside is too loud.

Several conditions work together for the experience of a particular object. For example, when hearing-consciousness arises, it is kamma which produces the vipākacitta which is hearing, as well as the earsense which is the doorway and the physical base of hearing. If kamma had not produced earsense one could not hear. Sound which impinges on the earsense is experienced not only by hearing-consciousness but also by other cittas arising in a process, each having their own function while they experience sound. In each process of cittas javana-cittas arise which are, in the case of non-arahats, either kusala cittas or akusala cittas.

Cittas which experience objects are accompanied by different feelings. Seeing, hearing, smelling and tasting which are vipākacittas experiencing a pleasant or unpleasant object, are always accompanied by indifferent feeling. Often it is not known whether the object experienced by these cittas was pleasant or unpleasant, they fall away immediately. When a pleasant or unpleasant tangible object is experienced through the bodysense, the body-consciousness, which is vipākacitta, is not accompanied by indifferent feeling but by pleasant bodily feeling or by painful bodily feeling. The impact of tangible object on the bodysense is more intense than the impact of the other sense objects on the corresponding senses. After the vipākacittas have fallen away javana-cittas arise. When these are kusala cittas they are accompanied by pleasant feeling or by indifferent feeling, and when these are akusala cittas they are accompanied by pleasant feeling, unpleasant feeling or indifferent feeling.

When we are not engaged with what is wholesome, javana-cittas which are akusala have the opportunity to arise. Hearing-consciousness may arise at this moment and we may not notice that clinging arises shortly afterwards. Clinging is bound to arise time and again. We think of what was seen, heard or experienced through the other senses most of the time with akusala cittas. There are many moments of ignorance when we do not even realize that we are thinking. However, citta thinks time and again of one object or another. When one has not studied the Dhamma one confuses the different doorways and the different objects, one "joins" them together. One is inclined to believe that there is a self who experiences a "thing" which lasts.

Only one object can be experienced at a time. We may wonder why we experience a particular object and why we shift our attention from one object to another. The "Atthasālinī" (Expositor II, Book II, Part I, Ch III, 333, 334) explains that the rūpas which can be experienced through the senses become objects "by virtue of deliberate inclination" or "by virtue of intrusion". We should remember that even following our own inclination is conditioned; that there is no self who can determine what kind of object is to be experienced. The "Atthasālinī" gives examples of experiencing an object with "deliberate inclination": when the bowl (of a monk) is filled with food and offered to him, one who takes up a lump and examines whether it is hard or soft, is considering only the element of solidity, although heat as well as motion are present[2]. As an example of the experience of an object "by virtue of intrusion", the "Atthasālinī" states that he who slips, knocks his head against a tree or in eating bites on a stone, takes as object only solidity, on account of its intrusiveness, although heat and motion are present as well. Further on the "Atthasālinī states:

> "But how does the mind shift from an object? In one of two ways:- by one's wish, or by excess of (a new) object. To expand: - one who goes to festivities held in honour of monasteries, etc., with the express wish of paying homage to the various shrines, to bhikkhus, images, and of seeing the works of carving and painting, and when he has paid his respects and seen one shrine or image, has a desire to pay homage to, and see another, and goes off. This is shifting by one's wish. And one who stands gazing at a great shrine like a silver mountain peak, when subsequently a full orchestra begins to play, releases the visible object and shifts to audible object; when flowers or scents possessing delightful odour are brought, he releases the audible object and shifts to the olfactory object. Thus the mind is said to shift owing to excess of (a new) object."

When we study and consider the Dhamma we may not hear the sound of traffic, but when the sound is very loud we may hear it. Then that object is intrusive. It is the same when we suffer from violent pains. Then there is an object which is intrusive, we cannot think of anything else but the pain.

Pleasant objects and unpleasant objects are experienced by kusala cittas and akusala cittas. Kusala citta as well as akusala citta can be object-condition for kusala citta or for akusala citta.

Kusala citta can be the object of kusala citta. We read in the "Paṭṭhāna" (Faultless Triplet, Kusala-ttika, VII, Investigation Chapter, pañha-vāra, Object, paragraph 404):

> "Faultless state (kusala dhamma) is related to faultless state by object-condition.
>
> After having offered the offering, having undertaken the precept, having fulfilled the duty of observance, (one) reviews it. Having emerged from jhāna, (one) reviews it. (One) reviews (such acts) formerly well done. Having emerged from jhāna, (one) reviews the jhāna. Learners[3]

---

[2] The four great Elements of solidity, cohesion, heat and motion always arise together, but only one rūpa at a time can be experienced. Solidity, heat and motion are tangible object, but cohesion cannot be experienced through the bodysense, only through the mind-door.

[3] The "learner", sekha, is the ariyan who is not arahat.

> review change-of-lineage[4]. (They) review purification[5]. Learners, having emerged from the Path, review the Path[6]. Learners or common worldlings practise insight into impermanence, suffering and impersonality of the faultless (state)..."

Kusala can also be the object of akusala citta. We read in paragraph 405:

> "Faultless state (kusala dhamma) is related to faulty state (akusala dhamma) by object-condition.
>
> After having offered the offering, having undertaken the precept, having fulfilled the duty of observance, (one) enjoys and delights in it. Taking it as object, arises lust, arise wrong views, arises doubt, arises restlessness, arises grief.
>
> Having emerged from jhāna, (one) enjoys and delights in the jhāna. Taking it (jhāna) as object, arises lust, arise wrong views, arises doubt, arises restlessness. When jhāna has disappeared, (one) regrets it and thereby arises grief..."

We should consider how object-condition operates in our daily life. Is it not true that we cling to our kusala, that we have conceit on account of it, that we find ourselves better than other people? We may take the performing of kusala for self. Or we may think of it with dosa. We may think of a generous deed with regret because we find that the gift we bought was too expensive. We have accumulated akusala and it will always find an object, even kusala.

We read in the same section of the "Paṭṭhāna" (paragraph 407) that akusala can be the object of akusala citta:

> "Faulty state is related to faulty state by object condition. (One) enjoys and delights in lust. Taking it as object, arises lust, arise wrong views, arises doubt, arises restlessness, arises grief..."

Don't we like lobha and enjoy having it? We want to have as many moments of enjoyment as possible. Then more lobha arises. If we do not realize lobha as a conditioned reality we take it for "my lobha". Lobha can also be object of dosa. We may feel guilty about lobha, we may have aversion towards it and we may regret it. Any kind of defilement can be object of akusala citta.

Akusala can also be object of kusala citta, for example, when we consider defilements with right understanding and realize them as conditioned realities which are not self. We read in the same section of the "Paṭṭhāna" (paragraph 408):

> "Faulty state is related to faultless state by object condition.
>
> Learners review the eradicated defilements. They review the uneradicated defilements. They know the defilements addicted to before.

---

4 Gotrabhū, the mahā-kusala citta accompanied by paññā preceding the magga-citta of the sotāpanna. Gotta means clan. Gotrabhū refers to the person who will become of the ariyan lineage.

5 Vodāna, the mahā-kusala citta accompanied by paññā preceding the magga-citta of the three higher stages of enlightenment (Vis. XXII, 23, footnote 7).

6 After the lokuttara cittas which arose at the attainment of enlightenment have fallen away, mahā-kusala citta accompanied by paññā reviews the magga-citta, path-consciousness.

> Learners or common worldlings practise insight into the impermanence, suffering and impersonality of the faulty (state)..."

The arahat can review kusala citta and akusala citta which formerly arose with kiriyacitta, which is indeterminate (avyākata) dhamma. Then kusala dhamma and akusala dhamma condition indeterminate dhamma by way of object.

Nibbāna and the eight lokuttara cittas which experience nibbāna cannot be objects of clinging. The magga-cittas (lokuttara kusala cittas) of the different stages of enlightenment eradicate defilements and finally, at the stage of arahatship, they eradicate all kinds of clinging. We read in the "Paṭṭhāna" (Faultless Triplet, Investigation Chapter, Object, paragraph 410):

> "Learners review (lower) Fruition. (They) review Nibbāna. Nibbāna is related to change-of-lineage, purification, Path by object-condition."

Nibbāna is object-condition for the eight lokuttara cittas which experience it, namely, the four magga-cittas (path-consciousness, lokuttara kusala citta) and the four phala-cittas ("fruition", lokuttara vipākacitta) arising at the four stages of enlightenment.

Nibbāna is also object-condition for the "change-of lineage", gotrabhū, mahā-kusala citta accompanied by paññā, arising in the process when enlightenment is attained, which precedes the magga-citta of the sotāpanna and which is the first citta experiencing nibbāna. The mahā-kusala citta accompanied by paññā preceding the magga-cittas of the three higher stages of enlightenment is called "purification" (vodāna) and nibbāna is object-condition for this type of citta.

After the lokuttara cittas have fallen away, maha-kusala cittas accompanied by paññā in the case of the "learners", the ariyans who are not arahat, review nibbāna and these cittas are conditioned by nibbāna by way of object-condition. In the case of the arahat, mahā-kiriyacittas accompanied by paññā review nibbbāna and these cittas are conditioned by nibbāna by way of object-condition.

Concepts can be objects of kusala citta, akusala citta or kiriyacitta. We cling time and again to possessions, we want to have things such as money, clothes or cars. Concepts can condition akusala citta by way of object-condition. Clinging cannot be eradicated immediately, but we can develop understanding in order to see things as they really are.

Concepts such as a person or a car are real in conventional sense, they are not real in the ultimate sense. If we only pay attention to concepts we tend to cling more and more to them. We may consider them the goal of our life. Time and again we are absorbed in our thoughts about people and things we perceive and we do not pay attention to the cittas which think of such concepts at those moments and thus, we are ignorant about what is really going on. We may not realize that there is seeing-consciousness which experiences only what appears through the eyesense, visible object, and that there are other types of cittas which pay attention to shape and form and cling to concepts, ideas of persons and things which seem to last. We should not try to avoid thinking of concepts, they belong to daily life. We could not perform our tasks without thinking of concepts. However, when right understanding is being developed one comes to know that there is not a "self" who sees, recognizes, likes or dislikes. These are different moments of cittas which change all the time.

One will come to know when the object of citta is visible object and when a concept. A concept does not have a characteristic which can be directly experienced. When we think of a person, we think of a "whole" which seems to last, but what we take for a person consists of many different elements which arise and fall away. Hardness may appear when we touch what we call a person. Hardness is an ultimate reality with its own unchangeable characteristic. Hardness is always hardness, it can be directly experienced. We can denote it with different names, but its characteristic remains the same. We cannot avoid thinking of "people", that would be unnatural, but we should know that at some moments an ultimate reality such as hardness is experienced, and at other moments we think of a concept. The thinking itself is an ultimate reality with its own characteristic, and it can be known as it is: a conditioned reality which is not self. The arahat thinks about concepts but he does not cling, he thinks with kiriyacitta.

When we experience a pleasant object, attachment tends to arise, and when we experience an unpleasant object, aversion tends to arise. These objects condition akusala cittas by way of object-condition. We may believe that a particular object inevitably conditions akusala citta, but we may forget that there are other factors as well which condition cittas. When an object presents itself there can be wise attention or unwise attention to it; there is wise attention to the object when kusala javana-cittas arise, and there is unwise attention when akusala javana-cittas arise. We read in the "Discourse on all the Cankers" (Middle Length Sayings I, no. 2[7]) that the Buddha, while he was staying near Sāvatthī, in the Jeta Grove, spoke to the monks about the controlling of all the cankers. We read:

> "The uninstructed common man... does not know the things worthy of attention (manasikaranīye dhamme) nor those not worthy of attention (amanasikaranīye)..."

We read that he, therefore, fails to give attention to what is worthy of it and directs his attention to what is unworthy. The well-instructed disciple knows what is worthy of attention and what is not, and he acts accordingly. We read in the Commentary to this sutta (Papañcasūdanī) :

> "...There is nothing definite in the nature of the things (or objects) themselves that makes them worthy or unworthy of attention; but there is such definiteness in the manner (ākāra) of attention. A manner of attention that provides a basis for the arising of what is unwholesome or evil (akusala), that kind of attention should not be given (to the respective object); but the kind of attention that is the basis for the arising of the good and wholesome (kusala), that manner of attention should be given."

When someone gives us a delicious sweet, it seems that we cannot help liking it as soon as we taste it, and that attachment is bound to arise. Then there is unwise attention to the object. But there can be wise attention shortly afterwards, for example, when we truly appreciate the kindness of the giver. Or we may consider that flavour and the enjoyment of it do not last, that all realities are impermanent. When someone speaks harsh words to us the sound is an unpleasant object and we

[7] I am using the translation by Ven. Nyanaponika, "The Roots of Good and Evil" I, 6. Wheel 251/ 253, B.P.S. Kandy.

may have aversion towards it. Then there is unwise attention. There can be wise attention if we, instead of having aversion, see the benefit of having compassion with the person who spoke harsh words.

When aversion arises on account of violent pain, there is unwise attention. But there can be wise attention when we understand that pain is vipāka, produced by kamma, that it is unavoidable. We may consider the impermanence and frailty of the body. Mindfulness of whatever reality appears is most beneficial. Our body consists of different rūpa-elements, and when there is pain the characteristics of hardness or heat may appear. These can be very painful, but instead of thinking of "our pain" mindfulness of realities can arise. Then we can see that hardness or heat are rūpas which arise because of their own conditions and that there is no self who has power over them. Painful feeling is nāma which arises because of its own conditions, it is beyond control. When aversion towards pain arises, aversion can be the object of mindfulness so that it can be seen as only a conditioned nāma. Only by right understanding of realities, clinging to "my body" or "my mind" can decrease. At the moment of right understanding there is truly wise attention.

We should not only consider object-condition but also the other kinds of conditions which have been classified in the "Paṭṭhāna", so that we shall understand the meaning of anattā, non-self. The teaching about conditions is not theory; conditioning realities and conditioned realities pertain to our daily life right now.

If we have more understanding of the object that presents itself now we shall also understand object-condition. Hardness may present itself at this moment through the body-door, and then hardness is object-condition for the body-consciousness that experiences it, and if this is followed by sati and paññā, hardness is object-condition for sati and paññā. But nobody can manipulate object-condition. Who knows what the next object will be and for which type of citta it will be object-condition?

When we consider object-condition we can be reminded to be aware of whatever reality presents itself, no matter whether it is a pleasant object or an unpleasant object, no matter whether it is kusala dhamma or akusala dhamma. We attach great importance to the kind of object we experience, but all our experiences are conditioned, beyond control.

4 Predominance-Condition

We read in the"Paṭṭhāna" (II, Analytical Exposition, 3) about two kinds of predominance-condition:

- conascent-predominance-condition (sahajātādhipati-paccaya)
- object-predominance-condition (ārammaṇādhipati-paccaya)

As to conascent-predominance-condition, the conditioning factor (paccaya) which has a dominating influence over the realities it conditions (paccayupanna dhammas) is conascent with these, that is, it arises together with them. Phenomena never arise alone, they arise simultaneously with other phenomena. Citta does not arise alone, it is accompanied by cetasikas; citta and cetasikas arise together and fall away together.

There are four factors which condition the dhammas they arise together with by way of conascent-predominance-condition, and these are:

- chanda (desire-to-do)[1]
- viriya (energy or effort)
- citta
- vimaṃsa (investigation of Dhamma, paññā cetasika)

Three of these factors, namely, chanda, viriya and vimaṃsa are cetasikas and one is citta, but not every citta can be a predominant factor as we shall see. It is due to these four factors that great and difficult enterprises can be accomplished. Whenever we wish to accomplish a task, one of these four factors can be the leader, the predominance-condition for the realities they arise together with and also for the rūpa which is produced at that moment by citta[2]. Only one of these four factors at a time can be predominant. For example, when chanda is foremost, the other three factors cannot be predominant at the same time. Chanda, viriya and citta can be predominant in the accomplishment of an enterprise or task both in a wholesome way and in an unwholesome way, whereas vimaṃsa, investigation of Dhamma, which is paññā, a sobhana cetasika, can only be predominant in a wholesome way.

The conascent predominant factors can operate at the moments of javana-cittas (kusala cittas or akusala cittas in the case of non-arahats)[3]. Kusala cittas are always accompanied by the two beautiful roots (sobhana hetus) of non-attachment (alobha) and non-aversion (adosa) and, in addition, they can be accompanied by paññā. Akusala cittas can be accompanied by two akusala roots: by ignorance (moha)

[1] Chanda is a cetasika which arises with cittas of the four jātis, but it does not arise with every citta. It accompanies kusala citta as well as akusala citta. It is translated as wish-to-do, desire or zeal.

[2] As we have seen, citta is one of the factors which produces rūpas of the body.

[3] The javana-cittas arise in the sense-door processes of cittas and in the mind-door process, and they "run through the object". There are usually seven javana-cittas in a process of cittas, and these are kusala cittas or akusala cittas. Arahats do not have kusala cittas or akusala cittas, they have kiriyacittas which perform the function of javana.

and attachment (lobha) or by ignorance and aversion (dosa), or they may have ignorance as their only root. There are two types of akusala cittas which have moha, ignorance, as their only root: moha-mūla-citta (rooted in moha) accompanied by uddhacca (rest- lessness) and moha-mūla-citta accompanied by doubt (vicikicchā) and these cittas are weak compared to the akusala cittas that have two akusala hetus.

The conascent predominant factors do not operate in the case of these two moha-mūlacittas, they only operate in the case of javana-cittas that are accompanied by two or three roots.

When one undertakes a work of art, such as painting, or when one applies oneself to music, one is bound to do so with lobha-mūla-citta (citta rooted in attachment). Lobha is attached to the object it experiences, but it cannot accomplish anything, it is not a predominant factor. Chanda, zeal or wish-to-do, which accompanies lobha-mūla-citta can be a predominant factor in the accomplishment of one's undertakings, it conditions the citta and the other cetasikas it accompanies by way of conascent-predominance. When we are generous and like to give something away, chanda, which is kusala in this case, may be predominant. The kusala citta is also accompanied by alobha, non-attachment, and adosa, non-aversion or kindness, but these wholesome roots cannot be predominant in the accomplishment of a generous deed. It is chanda which can be predominant in the accomplishment of the generous deed, for example, when one chooses the gift and hands it to someone else.

Viriya can be a predominant factor in the accomplishment of our tasks. Preparing food may be part of our daily chores, and sometimes, when we like to do this, chanda may be predominant. At other times we may find it an effort but we may still want to cook. Then we may prepare food with viriya as predominant factor. At such moments there is likely to be lobha, but viriya is foremost in the accomplishment of cooking.

Citta can be a predominance-condition for the accompanying cetasikas, but not all cittas can be predominance-condition. As we have seen, predominance-condition can operate only in the case of javana-cittas accompanied by at least two roots. Moha-mūla-citta, which has moha as its only root cannot be predominance-condition, it has no strength to accomplish any task. Lobha-mūla-citta and dosa-mūla-citta which each have two roots (respectively moha and lobha, and moha and dosa), can be predominance-condition: they have a dominating influence over the accompanying cetasikas in the fulfilling of a task or enterprise in an unwholesome way. All mahā-kusala cittas (kusala cittas of the sense-sphere) and all mahā-kiriyacittas (of the arahat), have the two roots of alobha, non-attachment, and adosa, non- aversion, and, in addition, they can have the root which is paññā, thus, they have two or three roots and, therefore, they can be predominance-condition for the accompanying dhammas. When we accomplish a task with cittas which are resolute, firmly established in kusala, the citta can be the predominance-condition for the accompanying dhammas.

Jhānacittas (kusala jhānacitta and kiriya jhānacitta of the arahat), accompanied by the three roots of alobha, adosa and paññā, cannot arise without predominance-condition. The lokuttara cittas, the maggacittas and the phalacittas (lokuttara vipākacittas), accompanied by three roots, perform the function of javana; the phalacittas which immediately succeed the maggacittas are the only vipākacittas that perform the function of javana. Lokuttara cittas cannot arise without predominance-condition[4].

Lobha cetasika is not a predominant factor, but lobha-mūla-citta, citta rooted in attachment, can be predominance-condition, as we have seen. For example, when there is wrong view and wrong practice, the citta arising at that moment is firm and steady in this way of akusala, and then that citta is predominance-condition for the accompanying dhammas. That type of citta is rooted in moha and lobha and thus it is conditioned by these two roots by way of root-condition. When we abstain from slandering, the citta which is firm in kusala can be predominant, and in that case chanda, wish-to-do, and viriya, effort, are not predominant.

With regard to investigation of the Dhamma, vimaṃsa, this is paññā cetasika. When we listen to the Dhamma, consider it and are mindful of realities, vimaṃsa can condition the accompanying citta and cetasikas by way of predominance-condition.

The rūpas produced by citta can also be conditioned by way of predominance-condition. Body intimation (kāya-viññatti) and speech intimation (vacī-viññatti) are rūpas produced by citta[5]. When we present food to the monks, citta which is firm in kusala can be the predominant factor. While we, at such an occasion, show by our gestures our intention to give, there are rūpas which are body intimation, and these are conditioned by kusala citta by way of predominance-condition. When we slander, the citta which is firm in akusala may be predominance-condition, and the rūpa which is speech intimation is conditioned by the akusala citta by way of predominance-condition.

For the attainment of jhāna the predominant factors are necessary conditions, and in that case they have to be sobhana. It is extremely difficult to develop samatha to the degree of jhāna, and without the conditioning force of one of the four predominant factors one would not be able to attain jhāna. We read in the "Visuddhimagga" (III,24):

> "...If a bhikkhu obtains concentration, obtains unification of mind, by making zeal (chanda) predominant, this is called concentration due to zeal. If... by making energy predominant, this is called concentration due to energy. If... by making (natural purity of) citta predominant, this is called concentration due to citta. If... by making inquiry (vimaṃsa) predominant, this is called concentration due to inquiry (Vibhanga 216-219)..."

Predominant factors can be of different degrees. When the four factors mentioned above have been developed to a high degree, they have become "bases of success", iddhipādas, and then they can lead to the acquisition of supernatural

---

[4] For details about the cittas which can be conascent-predominance-condition, see Appendix 2.

[5] Body-intimation is a kind of rūpa which conditions gestures and other movements of the body by which we express our intentions. Speech intimation is a rūpa which conditions speech sound by which we express our intentions.

powers (Visuddhimagga, Ch XII, 50-53)[6]. The rūpas produced by citta which exercises such powers are also conditioned by way of predominance-condition.

In the development of vipassanā, right understanding of nāma and rūpa, one also needs the "four bases of success" for the realisation of the stages of insight wisdom and for the attainment of enlightenment. The arising of awareness and understanding of realities is beyond control, it is due to conditions. We need patience and courage to persevere studying and considering nāma and rūpa, and to be aware of them in daily life. For the accomplishment of our task, the development of right understanding, the factors which are predominance-condition are indispensable. The study of the predomi-nance-condition can be a reminder that right understanding is dependent on different kinds of conditions, that it does not depend on a "self". We read in the "Kindred Sayings" (V, Mahā-vagga, Book VII, Kindred Sayings on the Bases of Psychic Power (Iddhipādas, Bases of Success), Ch I, 2, Neglected):

> "By whomsoever, monks, the four bases of psychic power are neglected, by them also is neglected the ariyan way that goes on to the utter destruction of dukkha. By whomsoever, monks, the four bases of psychic power are undertaken, by them also is undertaken the ariyan way that goes on to the utter destruction of dukkha..."

It is then explained what the four bases of psychic power (iddhipādas) are. They arise together with right concentration and with right effort. Right effort in vipassanā is right effort to be aware of whatever reality appears at this moment.

As we have seen, there are two kinds of predominance-condition: conascent-predominance-condition and object-predominance-condition. In the case of conascent-predominance-condition the conditioning factor arises simultaneously with the conditioned dhammas, but this is not so with object-predominance-condition. As regards object-predominance-condition (ārammaṇādhipati-paccaya), not every object citta experiences is object-predominance-condition. An object which is predominance-condition is highly regarded by citta and the accompanying cetasikas so that they give preponderance to it. The predominant object is the conditioning factor (paccaya), and the citta and cetasikas which experience that object are the conditioned dhammas (paccayupanna dhammas). Object-predominance-condition is different from object-condition. For example, when we like the colour of a certain cloth, but we do not particularly want to possess it, that object conditions the lobha-mūla-citta by way of object-condition. When we like that cloth very much and want to possess it, that object conditions the lobha-mūla-citta by way of object-predominance-condition. We then give preponderance to that object.

Certain objects cannot be object-predominance-condition, because they are undesirable. Among them is the type of body-consciousness which is akusala vipāka, accompanied by painful feeling[7]. The two types of dosa-mūla-citta (one type un-

---

[6] Powers developed by means of samatha, such as walking on water, knowing one's former lives, etc.

[7] Body-consciousness is vipākacitta which experiences pleasant or unpleasant tangible objects. When it is kusala vipāka it is accompanied by pleasant bodily feeling and when it is akusala vipāka it is accompanied by unpleasant bodily feeling.

prompted and one type prompted, c.f. Appendix 2) cannot be object-predominance-condition. They are accompanied by unpleasant feeling and thus they are not desirable. The two types of moha-mūla-citta, one associated with doubt and one associated with restlessness, cannot be object-predominance-condition, they are not desirable. The akusala cetasikas which accompany dosa-mūla-citta and moha-mūla-citta are not desirable either, thus, they cannot be object-predominance-condition. One could not esteem regret, jealousy or stinginess, akusala cetasikas which may accompany dosa-mūla-citta.

We read in the "Paṭṭhāna" (Faultless Triplet, VII, Investigation Chapter, Conditions: Positive, 1, Classification Chapter, Predominance, 10, paragraph 413):

> "... After having offered the offering, having undertaken the precept, having fulfilled the duty of observance, (one) esteems and reviews it. (One) esteems and reviews (such acts) formerly well done..."

Wholesomeness can be object-predominance-condition for kusala citta which esteems and considers the wholesome deed which was done. In this case one gives preponderance to that object. When we have been generous we can recollect our generosity and this is a condition for the arising of other kusala cittas.

We read in the same section (paragraph 414) that dāna, sīla and jhāna can be object-predominance-condition also for akusala citta. When we have performed generous deeds with kusala citta we may find that citta highly desirable, we may be pleased with our own generosity. There may be attachment and wrong view on account of our good deeds. If we do not know the different conditions for kusala citta and akusala citta we may take for kusala what is actually akusala. Thus, kusala can be object of clinging, it can even be object-predominance-condition for clinging. Anything can be object of clinging, except nibbāna and the eight lokuttara cittas which experience it. As we have seen (in Ch 2), lokuttara dhammas cannot be object-condition for lobha-mūla-citta; neither can they be object-predominance-condition for lobha-mūla-citta.

Nibbāna is object-predominance-condition for the eight lokuttara cittas that experience it[8]. Nibbāna is object-predominance-condition for the "change-of lineage", gotrabhū, arising in the process when enlightenment is attained, preceding the magga-citta of the sotāpanna, and for the "purification" (vodāna) preceding the magga-cittas of the three higher stages of enlightenment[9].

Nibbāna and lokuttara cittas are object-predominance-condition for the mahā-kusala cittas and mahā-kiriyacittas (of the arahat) which arise after the attainment of enlightenment and which review, consider with paññā, nibbāna and the lokuttara cittas which arose.

Akusala can condition akusala citta by way of object-predominance-condition. We read in the "Paṭṭhāna", in the same section, paragraph 415:

---

8 Nibbāna is object-condition and object-predominance-condition for the cittas that experience it. Dhammas can condition other dhammas by way of more than one condition at a time.

9 The change-of-lineage and the purification are mahā-kusala cittas accompanied by paññā experiencing nibbāna, and these arise in the process when enlightenment is attained.

> "(One) esteems, enjoys and delights in lust. Taking it as estimable object, arises lust, arises wrong views. (One) esteems, enjoys and delights in wrong views. Taking it as estimable object, arises lust, arise wrong views."

If someone does not see the danger of lobha, he considers it the goal of his life to have as much enjoyment as possible. We like to enjoy nature, to buy beautiful clothes, to eat delicious food, to hear nice music. We like to enjoy all the pleasant things of life. It is natural that we enjoy pleasant things, but we can also develop right understanding of the different cittas which arise in daily life.

Pleasant sense objects are desirable and they can condition lobha-mūla-citta by way of object-predominance-condition. It may happen that we have many duties to do but that we are so carried away by the sound of music that we leave our duties and play the piano or go to a concert. Then we give preponderance to sound and this is object-predominance-condition for lobha-mūla-citta. This happens time and again in our daily life. We should not pretend that we do not have lobha, we should come to know our inclinations as they are. When lobha has arisen already because of its own conditions, we should not ignore it, but we can develop right understanding of it. When there is mindfulness of lobha when it appears, it can be known as a conditioned nāma, not self.

We read in the "Paṭṭhāna" (in the same section, paragraph 416):

> "(One) esteems, enjoys and delights in the eye... ear... nose... tongue... body... visible object... sound... smell... taste... tangible object... (heart-)base... Taking it as estimable object, arises lust, arises wrong views..."

The rūpas which have their own distinct nature[10] can be object-predominance-condition. Rūpa which is a desirable object can be object-predominance-condition only for lobha-mūla-citta. Rūpa cannot condition kusala citta by way of object-predominance-condition, only by way of object-condition. For example, if we want to give beautiful flowers to someone else, rūpa, such as colour or odour, can condition kusala citta by way of object-condition; rūpa is the object experienced by kusala citta. That rūpa cannot be object-predominance-condition for kusala citta. If one gives preponderance to it and wants to have it again and again it is object-predominance-condition for lobha-mūlacitta, but not for kusala citta. Kusala citta is accompanied by detachment, alobha, it is intent on letting go of objects.

The kusala one has performed before, such as generosity, may be object-predominance-condition for kusala citta, it can be a condition for kusala cittas to arise again. The development of kusala is conditioned by kusala accumulated in the past, and also by the factors of chanda (wish-to-do), viriya (effort), citta

[10] These are sabhāva rūpas. "Bhāva" means nature and "sa" can mean own. Sabhāva rūpas are rūpas with their own distinct nature. There are also asabhāva rūpas, which are not rūpas with their own distinct nature but which are special qualities or characteristics connected with other rūpas. Sabhāva rūpas are, for example, the four great Elements, the sense objects and the sense organs. Asabhāva rūpas, rūpas which do not have their own distinct nature, are, for example, the special qualities of rūpa which are lightness, pliancy and wieldiness. Or the four characteristics of rūpa which are origination, continuation, decay and impermanence of rūpa.

and vimaṃsa (investigation of the Dhamma), which are conascent-predominance-conditions.

We should find out to which objects we give preponderance. We should know whether they condition kusala citta or lobha-mūla-citta. It is important to realize in which way objects can condition different cittas. When lobha-mūla-citta arises the object it experiences may condition that citta only by way of object-condition or it may condition it by way of object-predominance as well. At different moments different conditions play their part in our life. Kusala can condition wrong view or conceit by way of object-predominance-condition: we may attach great importance to the notion of "my kusala" with wrong view. Or we may have a high esteem of our good deeds with conceit, while we compare ourselves with others.

When we are attached to colourful pictures our attachment may be object-predominance-condition for lobha-mūla-cittas; we may be quite absorbed in our enjoyment and forgetful of the development of right understanding. At other moments we may devote time to the study and the consideration of the Dhamma so that right understanding can develop. The Dhamma we hear may condition mahā-kusala citta accompanied by paññā by way of object-predominance-condition. We read in the "Lesser Discourse on the Destruction of Craving" (Middle Length Sayings I, no. 37) that Sakka, lord of the devas, had inclinations to mental development, but when there were conditions to enjoy sense-pleasures, he was absorbed in those. We read that Sakka asked the Buddha, who was staying near Savatthī in the Eastern Monastery, to what extent a monk comes to be completely freed by the destruction of craving. The Buddha answered:

> "As to this, lord of devas, a monk comes to hear: It is not fitting that there should be inclination towards any (mental-physical) conditions'[11]. If, lord of devas, a monk comes to hear this, that It is not fitting that there should be any inclination towards any (mental-physical) conditions', he knows all the conditions thoroughly, he knows all the conditions accurately; by knowing all the conditions accurately, whatever feeling he feels, pleasant or painful or neither painful nor pleasant, he abides viewing impermanence, he abides viewing dispassion, he abides viewing stopping, he abides viewing renunciation in regard to those feelings."

We then read that when he is so abiding he grasps after nothing in the world and attains arahatship. Sakka rejoiced in what the Buddha had said and after having given thanks he vanished. Moggallāna wanted to find out whether Sakka had grasped the meaning of the Buddha's words and to this end he appeared among the "devas of the Thirtythree". Sakka, who was equipped and provided with five hundred deva-like musical instruments, was amusing himself. When he saw Moggallāna coming he stopped those instruments and welcomed Moggallāna. Moggallāna then asked Sakka to repeat the Buddha's words about freedom by the destruction of craving. Sakka answered:

> "I, my good Moggallāna, am very busy, there is much to be done by me; both on my own account there are things to be done, and there are also

[11] In the "Papañcasūdanī ", the Commentary to this sutta, it is stated that these are the five khandhas, the twelve sense-fields (āyātanas), the eighteen elements.

> (still more) things to be done for the devas of the Thirtythree. Further, my good Moggallāna, it was properly heard, properly learnt, properly attended to, properly reflected upon, so that it cannot vanish quickly. . . "

Sakka invited Moggallāna to come and see the delights of his splendid palace. Moggallāna thought that Sakka lived much too indolently and wanted to agitate him. By his supernatural power he made the palace tremble, shake and quake. Moggallāna asked Sakka again to repeat the Buddha's words and then Sakka did repeat them.

We may recognize ourselves in Sakka when he tries to find excuses not to consider the Dhamma. We also are inclined to think at times that we are too busy to develop right understanding of realities, to be aware of nāma and rūpa over and over again, until they are thoroughly understood. When Moggallāna agitated Sakka there were conditions for him to give preponderance to the development of right understanding. Our life is likewise. When we listen to the Dhamma or read the scriptures there can be conditions to give preponderance to the consideration of the Dhamma and the development of right understanding. When there is mindfulness of nāma and rūpa as they appear one at a time, they can eventually be known as they are: elements which are non-self.

5 Proximity and Contiguity-Condition

We may wonder why life goes on and on. Yesterday there were seeing, hearing and thinking, and today these realities occur again. Experiences occur time and again because there are conditions for them. Proximity-condition and contiguity-condition are conditions for cittas to arise again and again, in succession. Each citta with its associated cetasikas falls away and conditions the arising of the succeeding citta with its associated cetasikas. The next citta cannot arise if the preceding citta has not fallen away, there can be only one citta at a time. It is difficult to know the succession of the different cittas since they arise and fall away very rapidly. Attachment may arise in a sense-door process and then in the mind-door process[1], but, so long as there is no clear understanding of different realities, it seems that attachment can last for a while. In reality there are different cittas arising and falling away, succeeding one another because of proximity-condition and contiguity-condition.

Anantara (proximity) means: without interval. Anantara and samanantara (contiguity) are different in name, but the same in meaning (Visuddhimagga, XVII, 74). Citta conditions, after it has ceased, the arising of the subsequent citta, without interval; citta is anantara-paccaya for the next citta. Moreover, citta is samanantara-paccaya for the next citta; cittas follow upon one another in the proper way, in accordance with a fixed order in their subsequent arising. "Saṃ" in samanantara can mean right or proper. The rebirth-consciousness, for example, is not followed by seeing, but by the first bhavanga-citta in that life. The condition of samanantara-paccaya has been taught in addition to anantara paccaya for the benefit of the listeners who might have misunderstandings. Samanantara is sometimes translated as immediate contiguity.

The preceding citta is the condition, paccaya, for the arising of the subsequent citta which is the conditioned dhamma (paccayupanna dhamma). The conditions of proximity and of contiguity do not pertain to rūpa. Rūpa can be produced by four factors: by kamma, by citta, by nutrition and by temperature or heat. Rūpas arise and then fall away and so long as there are conditions new rūpas are produced by the four factors[2] .

---

[1] See Appendix 1.

[2] In some cases there can be temporary suspension of citta, and then only rūpas arise and fall away. Those who have developed samatha up to the fourth stage of arūpa-jhāna, the "Sphere of Neither Perception Nor Non-Perception " and who have also realized the stage of enlightenment of the anāgāmī, non-returner, and of the arahat, can attain "cessation" nirodha-samāpatti. This is the temporary suspension of citta, cetasikas and mind-produced rūpa. Rūpas produced by kamma, temperature and nutriment, in the case of human beings, and rūpas produced by kamma and temperature, in the case of beings in the Brahma plane, continue to arise. When they emerge from cessation, the first citta which arises is the phala-citta, fruition-consciousness (lokuttara vipākacitta), which has nibbāna as its object. For the anāgāmī it is the phala-citta of the anāgāmī and for the arahat it is the phala-citta of the arahat. This citta is conditioned by the preceding citta, the arūpa-jhānacitta of the fourth stage which occurred prior to cessation. Thus, the force of proximity is not destroyed by the temporary suspension

The rebirth-consciousness, paṭisandhi-citta, which is vipākacitta, conditions the arising of the succeeding citta, the first bhavanga-citta in that life, which is of the same type of citta as the rebirth-consciousness. The bhavanga-cittas which arise throughout life, in between the sense-door and the mind-door processes of cittas, are of the same type of citta[3]. When there is birth in an unhappy plane of existence, such as the animal plane, the rebirth-consciousness is akusala vipākacitta. Because of proximity-condition and contiguity-condition bhavanga-citta succeeds the rebirth-consciousness and this citta is also akusala vipākacitta. The bhavanga-citta is in accordance with that kind of birth, it could not be changed into kusala vipākacitta. When one is born with mahā-vipākacitta[4] acccompanied by the three sobhana hetus of alobha, non-attachment, adosa, non-aversion, and amoha or paññā, the succeeding bhavanga-citta is of the same type of citta as the rebirth-consciousness. The bhavanga-citta is conditioned by the rebirth-consciousness by way of proximity-condition and contiguity-condition. The person who is born with three sobhana hetus has the possibility to attain enlightenment in that life if paññā is developed. Because of proximity-condition and contiguity-condition the potentialities one is born with are carried on from moment to moment.

Besides bhavanga-cittas, there are also cittas arising in sense-door processes and mind-door processes which experience objects impinging on the six doors. In the course of life we experience happiness and sorrow, but we could not have such experiences if the rebirth-consciousness had not arisen and if this citta was not succeeded by the following cittas, bhavanga-cittas and cittas arising in sense-door processes and mind-door processes. Our life is an unbroken series of cittas, succeeding one another without interval.

The cittas which perform their functions in the different processes[5] succeed one another in a regular order. The sense-door adverting-consciousness, the first citta which arises in a sense-door process, is conditioned by the last bhavanga-citta arising before the sense-door process starts, by way of proximity-condition and contiguity-condition. The sense-door adverting-consciousness experiences an object different from the object the bhavanga-citta experiences; it adverts to the object which impinges on one of the senses and is then succeeded by one of the sense-cognitions (the five pairs, pañca-viññāṇas, one kusala vipākacitta and one

---

of citta. It is the same in the case of rebirth in the asañña-satta plane, the plane where there is only rūpa. When the lifespan in that plane is over and there is rebirth in the sensuous plane, the rebirth-consciousness is conditioned by the dying-consciousness which occurred prior to rebirth in the asañña-satta-plane. Thus, the force of proximity is not destroyed.

[3] Bhavanga-cittas do not experience the objects which impinge on the six doors and which are experienced by the cittas arising within processes. Bhavanga-cittas experience the same object as the rebirth-consciousness, and this object is the same as the object experienced shortly before the dying-consciousness in the previous life. The object which the bhavanga-citta experiences does not appear to us, we do not know it.

[4] Kusala vipākacitta of the sense sphere, accompanied by two or three sobhana hetus, beautiful roots.

[5] See Appendix 1 for these processes. One cannot understand the conditions of proximity and contiguity if one is not familiar with the processes of citta.

akusala vipākacitta, of seeing, hearing, etc.) which experiences that object. Seeing and hearing arise time and again, also now. Thus, we know that the conditions of proximity and contiguity still continue to operate. The sense-cognition, such as seeing or hearing, does not last, it falls away and conditions the arising of the next citta, the receiving-consciousness, sampaṭicchana-citta, which "receives" the object. This citta is succeeded by the investigating-consciousness, santīraṇa-citta, which investigates the object, and this again by the determining-consciousness, votthapana-citta which "determines" the object. The votthapana-citta, after it has determined the object, is, in the case of non-arahats, followed by akusala javana-cittas or kusala javana-cittas. There are usually seven types of javana-cittas in a process of cittas, performing the function of impulsion or "running through" the object. The javana-cittas may be succeeded by the registering-consciousness, tadārammaṇa-cittas, vipākacittas which "hang on" to the object. Each of these cittas is conditioned by the preceding citta by way of proximity and contiguity, and in its turn, each of them conditions the arising of the next citta in these ways. After the sense-door process has been completed there are bhavanga-cittas again and then the object can be experienced by cittas arising in a mind-door process. The mind-door adverting-consciousness which adverts to the object through the mind-door, is the first citta of the mind-door process. It is succeeded by javana-cittas (in the case of non-arahats akusala cittas or kusala cittas), and then registering-consciousness, tadārammaṇa-cittas may arise. The cittas arising within the different processes do so according to a particular order which is unchangeable; they succeed one another without any interval and this is conditioned by way of proximity and contiguity. The javana-cittas, for instance, cannot arise if, in the sense-door process, the determining-consciousness and, in the mind-door process, the mind-door adverting-consciousness has not arisen. This reminds us that there is no self who can cause the arising of particular cittas.

When the object which is experienced is rūpa, such as visible object or sound, it lasts as long as seventeen moments of citta[6]. Seventeen moments is still extremely short. The experience of visible object and sound seem to occur at the same time, but in reality several processes of cittas which experience these different objects have occurred. If insight has not been developed, one does not realize the falling away of citta and the arising of the succeeding citta. We find the experience of sense objects very important, but we should remember that these experiences are fleeting, insignificant. Only through satipaṭṭhāna the understanding can be developed which realizes the arising and falling away of realities. We are born in the human plane where we have the opportunity to hear the Dhamma and, since such opportunity is rare, we should not neglect the development of understanding of realities.

Throughout the cycle of birth and death the conditions of proximity and contiguity prevail with unbroken continuity. Because of the uninterrupted succession of cittas past lives condition the present life and evenso the present life will condition future lives. Each citta falls away completely, but it conditions the succeeding citta. Tendencies and inclinations we had in former lives have been accumulated

---

6 See Ch 2. This is so when a process of cittas runs its full course. A process, however, can be interrupted earlier. For details see Appendix 1.

from moment to moment up to the present. Since each citta which falls away conditions the succeeding citta we can accumulate skills, knowledge and wisdom. It is because of proximity-condition and contiguity-condition that we can remember past experiences, events which occurred many years ago.

Kammas, good and bad deeds, committed in the past are accumulated from moment to moment, from life to life, and they can produce their appropriate results later on, when it is the right time. Because of kamma which produces results, pleasant or unpleasant objects are experienced through the senses by cittas which arise within processes. We see pleasant and unpleasant objects; seeing is vipākacitta, produced by kamma. The eye-door adverting-consciousness which precedes seeing in the eye-door process is also a condition for seeing: it conditions seeing by way of proximity-condition and contiguity-condition. If there were no eye-door adverting-consciousness, seeing could not arise. Cittas arise and fall away succeeding one another continuously because of conditions and we never know what the next moment will bring. We may be surprised that we quite suddenly have to suffer great pain or an accident. We are surprised, because we do not see proximity-condition and contiguity-condition which occur all the time within the cycle of birth and death.

The rebirth-consciousness, paṭisandhi-citta, is vipākacitta produced by kamma. Kamma causes us to be born in particular circumstances, in a particular family, where there will be favorable conditions or unfavorable conditions to do good deeds and to develop right understanding. The rebirth-consciousness is preceded by the dying-consciousness, the last citta of the preceding life. Because of proximity-condition the dying-consciousness is succeeded without any interval by the rebirth-consciousness. If we understand the proximity-condition occurring now, at this moment, we shall also see that the last citta of this life conditions the first citta of the following life by way of proximity-condition. The dying-consciousness may arise in a happy plane of existence, such as the human plane, but it can be succeeded by the rebirth-consciousness arising in an unhappy plane.

After this life there will be another life, until one has attained arahatship. The dying-consciousness of the arahat is not proximity-condition for rebirth-consciousness. So long as we are in the cycle of birth and death and we have not attained the state of the sotāpanna (who has realized the first stage of enlightenment), we can still be subject to an unhappy rebirth.

In the "Kindred Sayings" (I, Sagāthā-vagga, Ch VII, Brahmin Suttas, 2, The Lay Adherents, paragraph 2, Udaya) we are reminded of rebirth with its toils and sufferings, again and again, until arahatship has been attained. We read that the Buddha, on three consecutive days, came with his bowl to Udaya who filled it with rice. After the third time Udaya critizised the Buddha for coming again and again. The Buddha answered:

> "Again, again is seed in furrow sown,
> Again, again the cloud-king sends down rain,
> Again, again the ploughmen plough the fields,
> Again, again comes corn into the realm,

Again, again do beggars go their round,
Again, again do generous donors give,
Again, again when many gifts are given,
Again, again the donors find their heaven.
Again, again the dairy-folk draw milk,
Again, again the calf its mother seeks,
Again, again we tire and toil anew,
Again, again the slow wits seek rebirth,
Again, again comes birth, and dying comes,
Again, again men bear us to the grave.

When once the man of broad insight that Path
Which brings no new becoming does attain,
Then is he no more born again, again."

We then read that Udaya expressed his appreciation of the Buddha's words and took refuge in the Triple Gem. He wanted to become a layfollower of the Buddha.

6 Conascence and Mutuality-Condition

In the case of conascence-condition, a conditioning dhamma, paccaya dhamma, on arising, causes the conditioned dhammas, paccayupanna dhammas, to arise simultaneously with it. The Pāli term sahajāta in sahajāta-paccaya, conascence-condition, means: that which has arisen together. In the case of proximity-condition and contiguity-condition, the conditioning dhamma arises previously to the conditioned dhamma.

We read in the "Visuddhimagga" (XVII, 77):

> "A dhamma which, while arising, assists (another dhamma) by making it arise together with itself is a conascence-condition, as a lamp is for illumination..."

For the explanation of conascence-condition the "Visuddhimagga" uses the simile of an oil lamp: when its flame appears the light, colour and heat are produced simultaneously with it. Light, colour and heat produced by the flame are not present before the flame appears nor after it dies out[1].

We read in the "Paṭṭhāna" (II, Analytical Exposition, 6, Conascence-condition) about different classes of phenomena, nāma and rūpa, mentioned in relation to conascence-condition. We read with regard to the first class:

> "The four immaterial aggregates (nāmakkhandhas) are mutually related to one another by conascence-condition."

Viññāṇakkhandha, citta, cannot arise without the three other nāmakkhandhas, namely: vedanākkhandha (feeling), saññākkhandha (remembrance or perception) and saṅkhārakkhandha (formations, the other cetasikas). Citta is different from cetasika, it does not feel or remember; citta is the "chief" in cognizing an object but it needs the accompanying cetasikas which share the same object and which each have their own task while they assist the citta. Citta cannot arise without cetasika and cetasika cannot arise without citta, they condition one another by conascence-condition. Citta needs for example the cetasika phassa, contact, which contacts the object so that citta can cognize it. Thus, citta is conditioned by phassa by way of conascence. Phassa is conditioned by citta and the accompanying cetasikas by way of conascence. When phassa accompanies akusala citta it is also akusala and when it accompanies kusala citta it is also kusala.

Each of the four nāmakkhandhas can be taken in turn as conditioning dhamma or as conditioned dhamma because they are mutually related by way of conascence. The "Paṭṭhāna" (Faultless Triplet, Ch VII, Investigation Chapter. Conditions: positive, 1, classification chapter, Conascence 9, paragraph 419) expresses this as follows:

> "Faultless state (kusala dhamma) is related to faultless state by conascence-condition.
>
> One faultless khandha is related to three (faultless) khandhas by conascence-condition; three khandhas are related to one khandha by conascence-condition; two khandhas are related to two khandhas by conascence-condition."

---

[1] See "Guide to Conditional Relations" Part I, p. 23, by U Nārada.

This pertains only to the four nāmakkhandhas. The same is said with regard to the four nāmakkhandhas which are akusala (faulty).

When lobha-mūla-citta, citta rooted in attachment, arises, the four nāmakkhandhas are akusala and they condition one another by way of conascence. Lobha-mūla-citta has as roots moha and lobha, and these roots condition the accompanying dhammas by way of conascence-condition and also by way of root-condition. Phenomena can condition other phenomena in several ways. Lobha-mūla-citta may be accompanied by pleasant feeling. Feeling is conditioned by citta and the accompanying cetasikas, and when it accompanies akusala citta it is also akusala. Pleasant feeling which is akusala has a characteristic which is quite different from pleasant feeling which is kusala. When we enjoy delicious food with pleasant feeling, that feeling is different from pleasant feeling arising when we appreciate someone else's kusala. In the latter case it is more refined and calm. There are many sobhana cetasikas accompanying kusala citta: calm, evenmindedness, confidence in kusala, mindfulness. They all condition the pleasant feeling that is kusala.

It is beneficial to learn more about conascence-condition because this condition pertains directly to our every day life. Citta and cetasikas which arise together condition one another mutually. When one, for example, develops understanding of nāma and rūpa, kusala citta is accompanied by paññā and by many other sobhana cetasikas. That citta is also accompanied by sati which is mindful of the reality which appears, by "applied thinking", vitakka[2], which "touches" the object so that paññā can understand it, by non-attachment, alobha, and by other cetasikas which each perform their own function. They all mutually support one another while they arise together. There are many degrees of paññā and as paññā grows it also supports the accompanying sobhana cetasikas. Alobha, non-attachment, for example, is still weak in the beginning, but as paññā develops, alobha also develops; this leads to more detachment from realities.

Citta and cetasikas can be of four "jātis" (classes), they can be kusala, akusala, vipāka or kiriya. Some cetasikas can accompany cittas of the four jātis, but in each case they are completely different because they are conditioned by the citta and the other cetasikas they accompany. Manasikāra, attention, for example, is a cetasika which arises with each citta, but it is quite different when it accompanies lobha-mūla-citta which clings to the object which is experienced, or when it accompanies kusala citta which is intent on generosity or on the observance of sīla. Viriya, energy or effort, can be energy for what is wholesome, or it can be energy exerted in an unwholesome way; effort can accompany kusala citta and akusala citta. One may make a great effort to obtain a beautiful gem one clings to, and this is different from the well-balanced effort that accompanies kusala citta.

Thus, there is a great variety of citta and cetasikas which mutually support one another. When we come to understand better the different conditions for the

---

[2] Vitakka cetasika arises with many cittas, but not with every citta. When it accompanies akusala citta it is wrong thinking and when it accompanies kusala citta it is right thinking. As a factor of the eightfold Path it is called "right thinking".

realities which arise, it will help us to see that there is no self who experiences objects, likes or dislikes them, or develops right understanding.

As to the second class of phenomena mentioned in relation to conascence-condition, we read in the "Paṭṭhāna" (Analytical Exposition, 6):

> "The four great primaries (Great Elements, mahā-bhūta rūpas) are mutually related to one another by conascence-condition."

The Elements of Earth (solidity), Water (cohesion), Fire (temperature) and Wind (motion) always arise together and condition one another. Rūpas of the body and rūpas of materiality outside arise and fall away in groups or units, and the four Great Elements are included in each group. Solidity is the foundation of the other three elements, temperature maintains the other three elements, cohesion holds them together and the element of motion[3] acts as their distension (Visuddhimagga XI, 109).

The "Paṭṭhāna" (Faultless Triplet, Investigation Chapter, paragraph 419, VII,c) states as to the way the four great Elements condition each other that one "great primary" conditions the other three, three condition one, and two condition two.

Every day we experience a great variety of sense objects, but they are, in fact, only different compositions of rūpa elements. When we touch a table or a piece of cloth, tangible object may appear, such as hardness or softness. Hardness, softness, heat, cold, motion or pressure can be experienced by touch[4]. We think that tangible object can last, but it is only rūpa which arises and falls away all the time.

As to the third class of phenomena mentioned in relation to conascence-condition, the paṭisandhi-citta arising in the five-khandha planes (where there are nāma and rūpa) and the rūpa which is the heart-base for the paṭisandhi-citta condition one another by way of conascence.

In the planes where there are nāma and rūpa, each citta needs a physical base (vatthu) or place of origin. The vatthu for seeing is the eye-base, and each of the sense-cognitions (the five pairs, pañca-viññāṇas, of which one is kusala vipākacitta and one akusala vipākacitta) has its corresponding base. The cittas other than the sense-cognitions have the heart-base as their vatthu. During life the rūpa which is the vatthu has to arise before the citta which is dependant on it since rūpa is too weak at its arising moment to function as base. However, at the moment of rebirth, citta and its physical base arise at the same time. At that moment kamma produces the heart-base at the same time as the paṭisandhi-citta which is the mental result of kamma, vipākacitta, and this citta arises at the heart-base. In the planes where there are nāma and rūpa the paṭisandhi-citta and the heart-base cannot arise without one other. They condition one another by way of conascence.

The heart-base is not the only rūpa produced by kamma at the first moment of our life. Kamma produces at that moment three groups of rūpa: one group with the heart-base, one group with the bodybase and one group with sex, masculinity

---

[3] Motion is not movement in conventional sense; this rūpa has the characteristic of motion or pressure. It is sometimes translated as oscillation or vibration. It causes distension, and this can be noticed, for example, when there is pressure of air in the stomach or abdomen.

[4] The element of cohesion cannot be experienced by touch.

or femininity. In each of these groups the eight inseparable rūpas[5] and life-faculty (jīvitindriya)[6] are included as well, and thus, at the moment of our birth, three groups of ten rūpas produced by kamma arise. Without the paṭisandhi-citta these groups could not arise at that moment. Thus, the paṭisandhi-citta is conascence-condition for the three groups of rūpas produced by kamma, but only the heart-base among these rūpas is conascence-condition for the paṭisandhi-citta; this citta could not arise without the heart-base.

As to the fourth class of phenomena mentioned in relation to conascence-condition, citta and its accompanying cetasikas condition the rūpa produced by them by way of conascence-condition.

Citta produces rūpa at its arising moment. Each moment of citta can be divided into three extremely short periods (Visuddhimagga XX, 26): the moment of its arising (uppāda khaṇa), the moment of presence (tiṭṭhikhaṇa) and the moment of dissolution (bhaṅga khaṇa). Citta can only produce rūpa at its arising moment, since it is too weak to do so at the moment of its presence and of its dissolution. Sixteen types of citta do not produce rūpa. They are: the paṭisandhi-citta, the sense-cognitions (the five pairs of seeing, hearing, etc.), the four arūpāvacara vipākacittas (of immaterial jhāna, arising in the arūpa-brahma-planes where there is no rūpa) and the dying-consciousness, cuti-citta, of the arahat. Apart from these cittas, all the other cittas produce rūpas of the body[7]. Akusala cittas and kusala cittas can, for example, produce bodily intimation (gestures by which we express our intentions) and speech intimation. Akusala cittas and kusala cittas can produce bodily features by which our moods are expressed, such as regret, anger or enjoyment. Dosa can produce frowns and lobha can produce laughter. When we decorate our house, when we dress ourselves or when we use cosmetics, do we realize which types of citta produce rūpas while we move our hands? We may not even realize that lobha-mūla-cittas produce rūpas at such moments. We cannot force ourselves to lead the life of a monk, a life without sense-pleasures, but through the Buddha's teaching of the Vinaya, the Suttanta and the Abhidhamma we can come to know the defilements that arise. It is instructive also for laypeople to read the "Vinaya", the Book of Discipline for the monks, because it is a faithful mirror and a constant reminder of the different defilements which arise in daily life and are usually not known. We read in the "Vinaya" that it is forbidden to monks to decorate dwellings and objects they use, or to beautify themselves, since that is indulgence in sense-pleasures. The text of the "Vinaya" (Book of Discipline V, Cullavagga, Ch V, 106) states:

> "Now at that time the group of six monks anointed their faces, they rubbed (paste) into their faces, they powdered their faces with chunam,

[5] The four Great Elements and in addition: colour, odour, flavour and nutritive essense. These eight are present in each group of rūpas.

[6] This rūpa is present in all groups produced by kamma, not in groups produced by citta, temperature or nutrition. It only arises with rūpas of the body, not with external materiality.

[7] As we have seen, rūpas of the body can be produced by four factors: by kamma, citta, nutrition and temperature.

they smeared their faces with red arsenic, they painted their limbs, they painted their faces, they painted their limbs and faces. People spread it about, saying, Like householders who enjoy pleasures of the senses'..."

We then read that the Buddha did not allow it and said that it would be an offence of wrong-doing if monks would do any of those things.

The "Book of Analysis"(Vibhaṇga, second Book of the Abhidhamma, Ch 17, Analysis of Small Items, paragraph 854) reminds us that it is vanity to decorate objects or one's body:

"Therein, what is personal vanity'? Decoration of the robes, decoration of the alms-bowl, decoration of the abode; the decoration, beautifying, taking pride in, adorning, cupidity, state of cupidity, act of personal vanity, personal vanity for this putrid body and for the external requisites. This is called personal vanity."

Laypeople still have conditions for a life with sense-pleasures, but right understanding of the realities which arise can be developed. Also while one adorns oneself, nāma and rūpa appear and there can be awareness of them. If we know that, in such cases, rūpa is conditioned by citta by way of conascence, it can help us to understand nāma and rūpa as conditioned elements.

Citta and cetasikas which produce rūpa at their arising moment condition rūpa by way of conascence, but mind-produced rūpa, such as speech intimation, does not reciprocally condition citta by way of conascence. The arising of citta does not depend on mind-produced rūpa.

As to the fifth group mentioned in relation to conascence-condition, the four Great Elements condition the derived rūpas (upādāya rūpas) by way of conascence, but the derived rūpas do not reciprocally condition the four Great Elements by way of conascence. There are twentyeight kinds of rūpa in all, and the "derived rūpas" are the twenty-four kinds of rūpa other than the four Great Elements of solidity, cohesion, temperature and motion. The derived rūpas are dependant on the four Great Elements, they cannot arise without them. When sound, for instance, arises, it needs solidity, cohesion, temperature and motion. We are attached to the body and to our possessions, but these are only rūpas, the four Great Elements and derived rūpas in different compositions, arising because of conditions.

There is a sixth group of phenomena mentioned in the same section of the "Analytical Exposition"of the "Paṭṭhāna" concerning conascence-condition, but this is actually a further explanation of the relation of the heart-base to the citta which arises at the heart-base. Throughout life the heart-base has to arise before the citta which is dependant on it. Also the sense-bases which are the physical bases for the sense-cognitions such as seeing or hearing, which arise throughout life, have to arise previously to the cittas which are dependant on them. Rūpa, at its arising moment is too weak to be base, and therefore, it can perform the function of base only after it has arisen. However, the moment of rebirth is the first moment of life and in that case kamma produces the heart-base and the paṭisandhi-citta which is dependant on it simultaneously. At that moment the paṭisandhi-citta and the heart-base condition one another by way of conascence. The "Paṭṭhāna" (II, Analytical Exposition, 6, VI) states about the relation between heart-base and the citta which is dependant on it as follows:

> "The material states (rūpa-dhammas) are sometimes related to the immaterial states (nāma-dhammas) by conascence-condition and are sometimes not related by conascence-condition."

Some of the phenomena which are related by conascence-condition are also related by mutuality-condition (aññamañña-paccaya). They condition one another reciprocally while they arise simultaneously. The realities that condition one another mutually, can, each of them, be in turn conditioning dhamma (paccaya) and conditioned dhamma (paccayupanna dhamma). We read in the "Visuddhimagga" (XVII, 78):

> "A state that assists by means of mutual arousing and consolidating is a mutuality-condition, as three sticks of a tripod give each other consolidating support."

Three sticks which are leaning against each other at the upper ends mutually support one another. Evenso the realities to which mutuality-condition pertains condition one another reciprocally. There are three classes of phenomena to which this condition pertains.

As to the first class, the four nāmakkhandhas which condition one another by way of conascence, also condition one another by way of mutuality. They support and consolidate one another.

As to the second class, the four Great Elements which are related to one another by conascence-condition are also related to one another by way of mutuality-condition. Solidity, cohesion, temperature and motion which arise together condition one another reciprocally and give each other mutual support.

As to the third class, the paṭisandhi-citta with the accompanying cetasikas and the heart-base arising simultaneously condition one another by way of mutuality. As we have seen, at the moment of rebirth kamma produces, apart from the group of rūpas with the heart-base, two other groups, namely the group with the body-base and the group with sex. There is no relation of mutuality between the latter two groups and the paṭisandhi-citta.

The other classes of phenomena which are related by conascence are not related by mutuality. The rūpa produced by citta is conditioned by that citta by way of conascence, but there is no relation of mutuality. That rūpa does not, in its turn, condition citta, it does not consolidate citta by way of mutuality-condition. The four Great Elements are conascent-condition for the derived rūpas, but there is no relation of mutuality; the derived rūpas do not consolidate the four Great Elements by way of mutuality-condition. Visible object or sound, which are derived rūpas, cannot arise without the four Great Elements, but the four Great Elements are not dependant on these rūpas. Thus we see that phenomena which are related by mutuality are also related by conascence, but that not all phenomena which are related by conascence are also related by mutuality.

7 Dependence-Condition

The dependence-condition, nissaya-paccaya, refers to realities which condition other realities by being their support or foundation. We read in the "Visuddhimagga" (XVII, 79) about dependence-condition, which is here translated as support-condition:

> "A state (dhamma) that assists in the mode of foundation and in the mode of support is a support-condition, as the earth is for trees, as canvas is for paintings, and so on."

This type of condition refers to phenomena which are conascent (arising together) with the phenomena they condition as well as to phenomena which have arisen previously to the phenomena they condition.

We read in the "Paṭṭhāna" (Analytical Exposition, 8) as to the dependence-condition for conascent phenomena:

> "1. The four immaterial khandhas are mutually related to one another by dependence-condition.
>
> 2. The four great Elements are mutually related to one another by dependence-condition.
>
> 3. At the moment of conception, nāma and rūpa are mutually related to one another by dependence-condition.
>
> 4. States, citta and cetasikas, are related to mind-produced rūpa by dependence condition.
>
> 5. The four Great Elements condition the derived rūpas by dependence-condition."

As to the first class, the four nāmakkhandhas are mutually related to one another by conascent dependence-condition: citta and cetasikas always arise together and they are depending on one another. Citta cannot arise without cetasikas and cetasikas cannot arise without citta. As we have seen, they are also related to one another by way of conascence, sahajāta, and by way of mutuality, aññamañña.

The teaching of dependence-condition, nissaya paccaya, reminds us that citta and cetasikas need one another to perform their functions. Citta is the "chief" in cognizing an object, and cetasikas share the same object while they perform each their own function. Feeling, vedanā, and remembrance, saññā, are cetasikas which arise with each citta. Citta is different from cetasika, it does not feel or remember; citta cognizes or knows the object. Through awareness and right understanding developed in vipassanā the difference between citta and cetasika can gradually be known. Without awareness and right understanding there will only be theoretical knowledge of the way citta and cetasika condition each other by dependence-condition.

When lobha-mūla-citta arises it is dependent on the accompanying cetasikas. The roots of moha and lobha condition that citta and the other cetasikas by way of root-condition, hetu-paccaya, and also by way of dependence-condition, nissaya-paccaya. Ignorance and attachment are a support for the lobha-mūla-citta. Chanda, desire-to-do, and viriya, energy, also accompany the lobha-mūla-citta and they are dependence-condition for this citta. Chanda can be predominance-condition, adhipati-paccaya, for the citta and cetasikas it accompanies while one tries to acquire something one clings to. Lobha-mūla-citta just cognizes the desirable object which presents itself, it needs chanda to accomplish something, such as acquiring the object. Viriya can also be predominant when one tries to obtain something.

When kusala citta arises, it is dependent on alobha, non-attachment, and adosa, non-aversion, and also on other cetasikas. It needs for example chanda and viriya for the performance of dāna, the observance of sīla or the development of right understanding. Each of the accompanying cetasikas which performs its own task supports citta and conditions it by way of dependence-condition.

As to the second class, the four great Elements which are the rūpas of solidity, cohesion, temperature and motion, condition one another by way of conascent dependence-condition, sahajāta-nissaya-paccaya. They are a support for one another. Solidity cannot arise without cohesion, temperature and motion, and this is also true for the other three great Elements. They also condition one another by way of conascence-condition, sahajāta-paccaya, and mutuality-condition, aññamañña-paccaya.

As to the third class, at the moment of birth the paṭisandhi-citta and the hadaya-vatthu (heart-base) are mutually related to one another by way of dependence. In the planes where there are five khandhas, nāma and rūpa, kamma produces the rūpa which is heart-base at the same time as the paṭisandhi-citta which arises at the heart-base. The paṭisandhi-citta and the heart-base support each other and they cannot arise without each other. They are also related by way of conascence, sahajāta and by way of mutuality, aññamañña.

As to the fourth class, citta and cetasikas are related to mind-produced rūpa by way of dependence-condition. As we have seen, citta is one of the four factors which produce rūpas of the body. Citta and its accompanying cetasikas are a support to the rūpa produced by them, but that rūpa does not reciprocally condition the citta and cetasikas by way of dependence. When we, for example, speak kind words, the rūpa which is speech intimation is conditioned by kusala citta and accompanying cetasikas by way of dependence-condition. If there are no conditions for the arising of kusala citta it is impossible to speak kindly.

As to the fifth class, the four great Elements condition the derived rūpas (upāda rūpas, the rūpas other than the four great Elements[1]) by way of dependence-condition, but the opposite does not apply. Odour is a derived rūpa. It cannot arise by itself, it needs solidity, cohesion, heat and motion. When odour is experienced through the nose, only odour appears, the other rūpas which arise together with it in one group are not experienced. Visible object which is experienced through the eyes and sound which is experienced through the ears need the four great Elements as a foundation, they are conditioned by them by way of dependence.

Some phenomena which condition other phenomena by way of dependence have arisen previously to the phenomena they condition and, at that moment, they have

[1] There are twentyeight types of rūpa in all. Apart from the four great Elements there are twenty-four rūpas which are the derived rūpas. Among them are for example colour, odour, flavour, nutritive essence, the eye-base, the other sense-bases and the heart-base.

not fallen away yet. These are the rūpas which serve as vatthus or bases for the cittas they condition. They cannot be base at their arising moment since they are then too weak. Rūpa can perform the function of vatthu only at the moment of its presence[2]. Thus, it must be prenascent, arisen previously to the citta it conditions by dependence-condition. As we have seen, only at the moment of birth the heart-base arises together with the paṭisandhi-citta and serves as its base, but throughout life it arises previously to the cittas for which it serves as base and it conditions them by way of prenascent dependence-condition[3]. We read in the "Paṭṭhāna" (Analytical Exposition, 8. Dependence Condition):

> "(vi)Eye-base is related to eye-consciousness element and its associated states by dependence-condition.
> (vii) Ear-base is related to ear-consciousness element and its associated states by dependence-condition.
> (viii) Nose-base is related to nose-consciousness element and its associated states by dependence-condition.
> (ix) Tongue-base is related to tongue-consciousness element and its associated states by dependence-condition.
> (x) Body-base is related to body-consciousness element and its associated states by dependence-condition."

The five sense-bases have to arise previously to the corresponding sense-cognitions they condition by way of dependence-condition. The previously arisen eyebase is related to seeing-consciousness and the accompanying cetasikas by way of prenascent dependence-condition. Without eyesense, which serves as physical base and doorway, seeing could not arise. The eyebase itself is also conditioned, it is produced by kamma, and it lasts only seventeen moments of citta, which is extremely short.

The body-base is all over the body and inside it, except in the hairs or tips of the nails. It is one of the conditions for experiencing tactile object. It arises and falls away. We cling to the notion of "my eyes", "my ears", "my bodysense", but they are only rūpas produced by kamma which fall away immediately.

The following sutta reminds us of the fact that conditioned realities are impermanent. They arise because of other conditioned realities that are impermanent and therefore, they also have to fall away. Eyesense and seeing, earsense and hearing are impermanent and not self. We read in the "Kindred Sayings" (IV, Saḷāyatana vagga, Third Fifty, Ch 4, The Chapter on Devadaha, paragraph 139, The personal, by way of condition):

> "The eye, monks, is impermanent. Whatever condition, whatever cause there be for the appearance of the eye, that also is impermanent. Owing to impermanence the eye has come into being, monks. How could the eye be permanent?

---

[2] Rūpa lasts as long as seventeen moments of citta. After its arising moment it lasts sixteen more moments, fifteen moments of its presence and then there is its dissolving moment.

[3] The vatthus are during life for the cittas they condition a base-prenascence-dependence-condition, vatthu-purejāta-nissaya-paccaya.

(And it is the same with the other organs of sense).
The mind is impermanent... Owing to impermanence the mind has come into being, monks. How could mind be permanent?
So seeing, the well-taught ariyan disciple is repelled by the eye... tongue... mind. Being repelled he lusts not for it... so that he realizes, for life in these conditions there is no hereafter.' "

8 Decisive Support-Condition (Part I)

Upanissaya-paccaya, which can be translated as decisive support-condition or strong dependence-condition, occurs when a phenomenon assists another phenomenon by being a powerful inducement[1]. There are three kinds of upanissaya-paccaya:

- decisive support-condition of object, ārammaṇūpanissaya-paccaya
- decisive support-condition of proximity, anantarūpanissaya-paccaya
- natural decisive support-condition, pakatūpanissaya- paccaya

As to strong dependence or decisive support-condition of object, the object is the paccaya, condition, for the citta which experiences it, the paccayupanna dhamma, conditioned dhamma, and that object conditions the citta by way of strong dependence. We see in the "Paṭṭhāna" (Faultless Triplet, VII, Investigation Chapter, Strong Dependence, paragraph 423), that the objects which are the conditioning factors are the same as in the case of object predominance-condition, ārammaṇādhipati paccaya (see Ch 3), thus, they have to be desirable objects. The cittas which are conditioned by way of decisive support of object are of the same type as in the case of object predominance-condition. Thus, the realities to which these two kinds of conditions pertain are the same, but there is a difference in the conditioning force of object predominance-condition and of decisive support-condition of object. In the case of object predominance-condition the desirable object is highly esteemed by the citta and cetasikas concerned so that they give preponderance to it. In the case of decisive support-condition of object the desirable object is a powerful inducement, a cogent reason, for the arising of the citta and cetasikas concerned, which are strongly dependent on that object. Desirable objects which are object predominance-condition can also, at the same time, be decisive support-condition of object, a powerful inducement for the arising of the cittas concerned. Phenomena can be conditioned by several types of conditions at the same time.

Certain objects cannot be object predominance-condition nor decisive support-condition of object, because they are undesirable. Among them is the type of body-consciousness which is akusala vipāka, accompanied by painful feeling. The two types of dosa-mūla-citta (one unprompted and one prompted) and the two types of moha-mūla-citta (one accompanied by doubt and one accompanied by restlessness) are not desirable objects and thus they cannot be decisive support-condition of object. The akusala cetasikas which accompany dosa-mūla-citta, such as regret, jealousy and stinginess, and those which accompany moha-mūla-citta are not desirable either, thus, they cannot be decisive support-condition of object.

Kusala such as dāna or sīla can be object predominance-condition for kusala citta which esteems and gives preponderance to the wholesome deed one performed. The wholesome deed can at the same time also be decisive support-condition of object, it can be a powerful inducement, a cogent reason, for the arising again and again of kusala citta which sees the benefit of kusala.

Kusala can condition attachment or wrong view by way of object predominance-condition, and it can also condition attachment and wrong view by way of decisive

[1] The Pāli term upa means strong or powerful, and nissaya means dependence or support.

support-condition of object. It is then a powerful inducement for the arising of attachment and wrong view.

Attachment can be object predominance-condition and also decisive support-condition of object, a powerful inducement for the arising of attachment again and again in the case of all those who have not eradicated attachment.

Akusala cannot be object predominance-condition nor decisive support-condition of object for kusala citta, since kusala citta cannot consider akusala with esteem and high regard.

Desirable rūpas which are object predominance-condition can also be decisive support-condition of object for lobha-mūla-citta. Beautiful colours or delicious flavours are a powerful inducement for the arising of lobha-mūla-citta wanting such objects again and again. As soon as delicious food is on the tongue its flavour is irresistable for attachment. Someone may highly regard the sound of music which is then object predominance-condition for lobha-mūla-citta. The sound of music can also be a decisive support-condition of object, a powerful inducement for the arising again and again of lobha-mūla-citta, for example, when someone dedicates his whole life to music.

The rūpas of the five sense-bases, the heart-base and the sense objects can be decisive support-condition of object for lobha-mūla-citta but, just as in the case of object predominance-condition, they cannot be decisive support-condition of object for kusala citta[2] .

Only the rūpas which each have their own distinctive nature and are produced by one of the four factors of kamma, citta, temperature or nutrition, can be object predominance-condition as well as decisive support-condition of object for lobha-mūla-citta[3].

The objects which are decisive support-condition are a powerful inducement, a cogent reason, for the arising of the cittas which experience them. However, we should remember that there are also other conditions for the arising of kusala cittas and of akusala cittas. It depends on someone's accumulated inclinations whether he has "wise attention" or "unwise attention" to an object. Which objects are powerful inducements for the arising of kusala citta and which objects for the arising of lobha-mūla-citta in our life? Most of the time we are intent on acquiring pleasant objects for ourselves, objects which can be a decisive support-condition for clinging. There can be awareness of the realities which appear, also of clinging. We should not ignore clinging or despise it as an object of awareness. It arises naturally in our daily life because there are still conditions for its arising. If we do not know its true nature, we will take it for self and then it cannot be eradicated.

Nibbāna is a lokuttara dhamma that is a decisive support-condition of object for the cittas that experience it. We read in the "Paṭṭhāna" (Faultless Triplet,

---

[2] See Ch 3. Kusala citta does not give preponderance, for example, to a pleasant sense object; it is accompanied by detachment, alobha. Thus, it is not strongly dependent on that rūpa as object.

[3] These are sabhāva rūpas (see Ch 3), such as the four great Elements, the sense objects and the sense organs. Asabhāva rūpas, rūpas which do not have their own distinct nature, cannot be decisive support-condition.

VII, Investigation Chapter, Conditions, Positive, Classification Chapter, Strong Dependence, paragraph 423), that nibbāna is related to the eight lokuttara cittas which experience it and also to mahā-kusala citta accompanied by paññā and mahā-kiriyacitta (of the arahat) accompanied by paññā, by way of decisive support-condition of object[4].

Nibbāna and the lokuttara cittas which experience it cannot be object predominance-condition for lobha-mūla citta, nor can they be decisive support-condition of object for lobha-mūla-citta.

As we have seen, the first condition classified under decisive support-condition is decisive support-condition of object. The second condition classified under decisive support-condition is decisive support-condition of proximity, anantarūpanissaya-paccaya. This condition is similar to proximity-condition. Each citta that arises and falls away conditions the following citta by way of proximity-condition without any interval (anantara-paccaya, see Ch 4). As to decisive support-condition of proximity, this is also related to each preceding citta which conditions the succeeding citta. However, a distinction between these two conditions has to be made. The teaching of decisive support-condition of proximity emphasizes the aspect of powerful inducement of the conditioning force in the relationship between the conditioning reality, the preceding citta, and the conditioned reality, the succeeding citta. Citta can arise without being conditioned by way of root-condition and other conditions, but not without being conditioned by the preceding citta. Thus, the preceding citta as conditioning factor is a powerful inducement or cogent reason for the arising of the succeeding citta (see "Visuddhimagga", Ch. XVII, 82).

The paṭisandhi-citta, for example, is a cogent reason for the succeeding bhavanga-citta, so that life can continue. If the preceding citta would not be a powerful inducement for the arising of the succeeding citta, there could not be a continuous succession of cittas, even at this moment. In the case of birth as an animal, the paṭisandhi-citta is akusala vipākacitta, and this citta conditions the succeeding bhavanga-citta by way of proximity decisive-support-condition. The bhavanga-citta is the same type of citta as the paṭi-sandhi-citta, it could not change into kusala vipākacitta. Birth as an animal is different from birth as a human being, and the bhavanga-citta which succeeds the paṭisandhi-citta in the case of these different kinds of births is the same type of vipākacitta as the paṭisandhi-citta. We can notice that the lives of animals and of human beings are completely different. Beings are born with different potentialities, different capabilities, and these are carried on to the succeeding bhavanga-citta and then to the following cittas which arise in succession throughout life. In between the processes of cittas there are bhavanga-cittas, and they are of the same type as the paṭisandhi-citta.

[4] There is one type of lokuttara kusala citta and one type of lokuttara vipākacitta arising in the case of each of the four stages of enlightenment, thus there are eight types of lokuttara citta. The mahā-kusala citta preceding lokuttara citta also experiences nibbāna. The cittas which review nibbāna, arising after the lokuttara cittas have fallen away, are mahā-kusala citta accompanied by paññā or mahā-kiriyacitta accompanied by paññā.

Each citta which arises falls away immediately, but it has a conditioning force which is a powerful inducement for the arising of the succeeding citta without any interval. Thus, good and bad qualities can be carried on from moment to moment, they can be accumulated. Attachment has been accumulated from life to life. We think time and again with attachment about honour and all the pleasant things we want to obtain for ourselves. We have an interest in the Dhamma because this has been accumulated. We may have listened to the Dhamma in past lives, but we do not remember this anymore. Interest in the Dhamma and also the inclination to develop right understanding can be carried on from life to life because of proximity decisive support-condition.

In the development of vipassanā, insight, awareness can arise of whatever reality appears at the present moment. Because of proximity-condition and of proximate decisive support-condition citta arises and falls away and is then succeeded by the next citta. At one moment seeing arises, at another moment attachment to visible object, at another moment again hearing or attachment to sound. Nobody can choose the object of awareness, because realities appear already because of their own conditions. Cittas which arise in a process of cittas do so according to a fixed order which cannot be changed. Each preceding citta is a powerful inducement for the arising of the next citta.

So long as we are in the cycle of birth and death there are conditions for each citta to be succeeded by the next citta. The development of right understanding of the different characteristics of realities as they appear one at a time will eventually lead to the end of the cycle. We confuse the different doorways of sense-doors and mind-door, we do not clearly distinguish be-tween different cittas which experience one object at a time through one doorway. Through the development of right understanding one learns that the doorways and the realities which are dependent on them are different. Seeing is completely different from hearing, it arises because of different conditions, it experiences an object different from the object which hearing experiences. The aim of the study of the conditions for the realities which arise is the understanding of the truth of non-self.

We read in the "Kindred Sayings"(IV, Saḷāyatana Vagga, Second Fifty, 5, The Chapter of the Six, paragraph 94, Including the sixfold sense-sphere) that the Buddha said that the lack of restraint of the six spheres of contact (the five senses and the mind) leads to dukkha, whereas their being well tamed, well watched, well restrained[5], leads to happiness. We read in the verse:

> He meets with dukkha, monks, who has not tamed
> The sixfold impact of the sphere of sense.
> They who have learned the mastery of these,
> With faith for comrade,- they dwell free from lust.
>
> Beholding with the eye delightful things

[5] We also read in other parts of the teachings that the six doors are "guarded" through satipaṭṭhāna. Only right understanding of the reality which appears can eventually eradicate defilements.

Or things unlovely, let him restrain his bent
To lust for loveliness, and let him not
Corrupt his heart with thoughts of "O, it is dear."

And when, again, sounds sweet or harsh he hears,
Not led astray by sweetness, let him check
The error of his senses. Let him not
Corrupt his heart with thoughts of "O, it is sweet."

If some delightful fragrance meet the nose,
And then again some foul malodorous stench,
Let him restrain repugnance for that stench,
Nor yet be led by lust for what is sweet.

Should he taste savours that are sweet and choice,
And then again what is bitter to the tongue,
He should not greedily devour the sweet,
Nor yet show loathing for the bitter taste.

By pleasures' impact not inebriate,
Nor yet distracted by the touch of pain,
To pain and pleasure both indifferent
Let him be free from likings and dislikes.

Obsessed (by lusts) are others: so obsessed
They know and so they fare. But he dispels
All the world's vulgar fashionings of mind.
And treads the path renunciation-bound.

By contact of these six, if mind be trained,
The heart is never shaken any more.
Overcome these two, O monks,- lust and hate.
Do you pass beyond the bounds of birth and death.

9 Decisive Support-Condition (Part II)

As we have seen, there are three kinds of decisive support-condition: decisive support of object, ārammaṇūpanissaya-paccaya, decisive support of proximity, anantarūpanissaya-paccaya, and natural decisive support-condition, pakatūpanissaya-paccaya.

With regard to the third decisive support-condition, the natural decisive support-condition, pakatūpanissaya-paccaya, the Commentary to the "Paṭṭhāna" (the Pañcappakaraṇatthakathā) explains the term "pakata" in pakatūpanissaya. Pakata means done properly, done thoroughly. Kusala and akusala which were "done thoroughly", often performed, can become firmly accumulated, they can become habitual. In this way they are a cogent reason, a powerful inducement for the arising of kusala and akusala later on, which are the dhammas conditioned by them, the paccayupanna dhammas. Also external conditions, such as temperature, food, dwelling place and friends one associates with can be cogent reasons for the dhammas which they cause to arise.

The Commentary defines in addition the term pakatūpanissaya, as natural condition, explaining the word "pakati" which is connected with "pakatūpanissaya", as naturally, by nature. The conditioning factor conditions the arising of other dhammas naturally, and it can condition them without the assistance of decisive support-condition of object or decisive support-condition of proximity. For example, when there is strong confidence (saddhā) in kusala, this can be a cogent reason for the arising of kusala citta later on, without the need to be dependent on decisive support-condition of object or decisive support-condition of proximity.

The "Paṭṭhāna" explains that kusala, which formerly arose, such as confidence, sīla, the study of the Dhamma and generosity, are natural decisive support-condition for their arising again, later on. We read in the "Paṭṭhāna" (Faultless Triplet, VII, Investigation Chapter, Conditions Positive, paragraph 423,c, Natural strong dependence):

> "By the strong dependence of confidence... of precept (sīla)... of learning... generosity... By the strong dependence of wisdom, (one) offers the offering, undertakes the precept, fulfils the duty of observance, develops jhāna, develops insight, develops Path, develops superknowledge, develops attainment. Confidence, precept, learning, generosity, wisdom is related to confidence, precept, learning, generosity, wisdom, by strong dependence condition."

Good and bad qualities accumulated in the past become our nature, they condition the different cittas in the present life by way of natural decisive support-condition. We read in the "Mahā-Sutasoma Jātaka" (Jātaka Stories V, no. 537) that the Buddha said that not only in his present life he had tamed the robber Aṅgulimāla who had slain many people but later on attained arahatship, but also in a former life when the Buddha was King Sutasoma and Aṅgulimāla was the King of Bārāṇasī. Once Aṅgulimāla's cook could not obtain meat and gave him, without telling him, human flesh. We read (458):

> "... No sooner was a bit of the meat placed on the tip of the King's tongue than it sent a thrill through the seven thousand nerves of taste and continued to create a disturbance throughout his whole body. Why was this? From his having previously resorted to this food..."

His longing for human flesh became exceedingly strong, it determined his whole life. He was unable to give up his craving, so he abandoned his kingdom and kept on murdering for the sake of human flesh. He had accumulated greed for human flesh because in his preceding life he had been a man-eating Yakkha. His previous accumulations were the natural decisive support-condition for the arising of greed for human flesh and for his killing of human beings. He could not refrain from taking human flesh. Thus we see that unwholesome deeds performed in the past are not only capable of producing unpleasant results later on, but that they can also be a natural decisive support-condition for the committing of unwholesome deeds at the present. Akusala kamma is dangerous because the tendency to akusala is accumulated to perform akusala kamma again.

We read in the same Jātaka that one day the King seized Sutasoma, the Bodhisatta. Sutasoma asked permission to be temporarily released in order to fulfill a promise he had made to a brahmin, and after he had done so he returned to the man-eater without fear, and preached to him. He said (491):

> "Of all the sweets this world can yield to me
> None sweeter than the joys of Truth I see:
> Brahmins and priests that in the Truth abide,
> Birth, death escaping, reach the further side."

The Bodhisatta said that he was willing to give up all his wealth, his limbs and his life for the sake of truth. He converted and tamed the man-eater. The perfections (pāramīs) he had accumulated conditioned his heroic attitude and his preference for the truth.

The Bodhisatta developed all the perfections during countless lives in order to attain Buddhahood. We may have accumulated an interest in the Dhamma, but the perfections have not been accumulated to the degree that the stages of insight can arise and that enlightenment can be attained. Mindfulness of realities does not often arise; its arising cannot be controlled by a "self", it is dependent on the right conditions. Not only right understanding, but also other wholesome qualities such as generosity, sīla, mettā and patience have to be developed. They are sobhana cetasikas, beautiful mental factors, which are saṇkhārakkhandha, the khandha of "formations"[1]. The different factors of which this khandha is composed mutually strengthen and support one another and they are accumulated so that there will be conditions for enlightenment in the future.

In the process of cittas leading to enlightenment, paññā realizes the true nature of the reality which appears, it realizes one of the three characteristics of that

---

[1] All cetasikas other than feeling and saññā, remembrance, are included in saṅkhārakkhandha.

reality, namely impermanence, dukkha or anattā. Only one of these three characteristics is realized at that moment because citta can have only one object at a time. However, before the three characteristics of reality can be known as they are, right understanding of all nāmas and rūpas which appear in daily life has to be gradually developed, and moreover, the "perfections" have to be accumulated. The accumulated perfections, paññā included, are the natural strong dependence-condition for the complete abandoning of all clinging to the wrong view of self when the first stage of enlightenment, the stage of the sotāpanna, is reached. Lokuttara citta cannot arise without the right conditions.

We read in the "Paṭṭhāna" (under Strong Dependence, paragraph 423):

> "The preparation for the first Path[2] is related to the first Path by (natural) strong dependence-condition."

The same is said with regard to the second, third and fourth Path. More- over, the first Path is related to the second Path by natural strong dependence, and it is the same with the subsequent Paths.

The natural decisive support-condition, pakatūpanissaya paccaya, includes many different aspects. Kusala citta that arose before can be a natural decisive support-condition for akusala citta arising afterwards; we may cling to the kusala we performed or we may have conceit about it. We read in the "Paṭṭhāna" (same section, paragraph 423, II b):

> "Confidence, precept, learning, generosity, wisdom is related to lust, hate, delusion, conceit, wrong views, wish, by (natural) strong dependence-condition."

Knowledge of the Dhamma may be a natural decisive support-condition for conceit or for wrong view. Someone may have studied the Dhamma but he may not consider nāma and rūpa appearing in daily life and have wrong understanding of the practice of vipassanā. Or someone may have confidence in a teacher who practises in the wrong way and thus he may follow the wrong practice.

Kusala can lead to aversion, it can be a natural decisive support-condition for aversion. When we make an effort to help someone else, that person may not appreciate our help and then we are likely to have aversion. If we do not study the different conditions we may not understand that the performing of good deeds can be a condition for the arising of akusala citta. If we do not develop satipaṭṭhāna with the purpose of eradicating akusala, the kusala we perform can, without our noticing it, be a natural decisive support-condition for akusala citta.

Kusala citta can lead to bodily discomfort, which is akusala vipākacitta. Someone may, for example, pay respect at the Buddhist holy places in India, and this is a wholesome deed. However, the hotel where he is staying may be dilapidated, without facilities, and this causes him to suffer from heat, mosquitos and other discomforts. The body-consciousness is in that case akusala vipāka produced by akusala kamma. However, it is also conditioned by kusala kamma by way of natu-

---

2 The magga-citta of the first stage of enlightenment, the stage of the "streamwinner", sotāpanna. There are four stages of enlightenment.

ral decisive support-condition. Phenomena which arise are not merely conditioned by one type of condition but by several types.

Accumulated unwholesome inclinations are a natural decisive support-condition for the arising of akusala citta at the present time. Accumulated dosa can lead to the killing of living beings. Also accumulated lobha can lead to killing, for example, when one kills because one wishes to have someone's property. At the moment of killing there is dosa-mūla-citta, but lobha can motivate the deed, it can be a natural decisive support-condition.

When one commits one kind of akusala it can easily lead to the committing of other types of akusala. We read in the "Paṭṭhāna"(same section, paragraph 423, IV, c):

> "Killing is related to killing... stealing... unlawful intercourse with the other sex... lying... slander... rude speech... foolish babble... avarice... ill-will... wrong views by strong dependence-condition."

It is then explained that stealing and the other kinds of evil are related to all kinds of akusala by way of decisive support-condition. We may think that it is not very harmful to indulge in idle, useless speech. However, this kind of speech can be a natural decisive support-condition for lying, stealing, killing or other kinds of akusala kamma.

Akusala can also be a natural decisive support-condition for kusala. Because of aversion towards akusala vipāka or attachment to kusala vipāka someone may perform good deeds. He may regret the akusala he performed in the past and then, in order to counteract it, he performs kusala. We read in the "Paṭṭhāna" (same section, paragraph 423, V):

> "After having killed, (one) offers the offering, undertakes the precept, fulfils the duty of observance, develops jhāna, develops insight, develops Path, develops superknowledge, develops attainment, to counteract it."

The same is said with regard to other kinds of evil deeds, they can be a natural decisive support-condition for kusala.

When kamma produces result, it is kamma-condition for that result, and, at the same time, it is also natural decisive support-condition, a cogent reason for that result to be produced. We performed many kinds of kamma also in past lives, and we do not know which kamma will produce result at a particular moment. When at this moment vipākacitta experiences a pleasant or an unpleasant object through one of the senses we know that kamma is a cogent reason, a decisive support-condition for such result. We are born in the human plane and therefore, we know that kusala kamma has produced the paṭisandhi-citta. Among the innumerable deeds done in the past that particular kamma has been a powerful inducement, a natural decisive support-condition for the paṭisandhi-citta. Kamma has by its own nature the power to cause the arising of the appropriate result, even after countless lives: it is kamma-condition as well as natural decisive support-condition for that result.

As we have seen, kusala kamma and akusala kamma performed in the past are also a natural decisive support-condition for kusala kamma and akusala kamma at the present time. Evenso by performing good or evil deeds now, we accumulate the tendency to perform similar deeds later on, thus, such actions are a natural decisive support-condition for future deeds.

The natural decisive support-condition comprises also vipāka which conditions akusala citta or kusala citta. Vipāka conditions kusala citta when, for example, we suffer bodily pain and we are then reminded that life is short and that we should not delay the development of right understanding. Vipāka conditions akusala citta when we have aversion towards bodily pain.

Kusala vipāka can be a condition for the arising of akusala vipāka later on, and akusala vipāka for the arising of kusala vipāka later on by way of natural decisive support-condition. Body-consciousness can be kusala vipākacitta or akusala vipākacitta. A painful massage conditions body-consciousness that is akusala vipākacitta, but it may lead to the alleviation of pain and to bodily wellbeing later on.

Natural decisive support-condition also comprises factors such as climate, food, dwelling-place, family and friends. We can notice that good and bad friends condition our spiritual progress or decline. Someone may be in the company of bad friends who induce him to take drugs or alcoholic drinks, but the same person may be at another time with a good friend in the Dhamma who explains the teachings to him. It depends on his accumulated inclinations whether he will continue to be with the wrong friends or with the right friends. It is beneficial to know our different accumulations and the different conditions which play their part in our life.

We can experience that bodily health or sickness conditions our cittas. Food, taken in the right amount, can be the condition for our ability to develop right understanding. The Buddha, before his enlightenment, fasted to the extent of becoming completed emaciated. He then understood that he was not practising the Middle Way and he took rice-gruel offered to him by Sujatā. On that day food was a natural decisive support-condition for the development of the right Path leading to his enlightenment. The right dwelling-place can also be a natural decisive support-condition for one's spiritual progress. Out of compassion the Buddha explained into the minutest details how dwelling-places should be kept and cleaned. He thought of the well-being of the monks. We read, for example, in the "Vinaya" (Book of the Discipline V, Culla-vagga, Ch VIII, On Observances, 208) that a monk should clear out an unoccupied dwelling-place and then clean it:

> "... If there are cobwebs in the dwelling-place, he should first remove them from the (floor-) covering. He should wipe the corners of the window-holes. If a wall that was coloured red becomes stained, he should wipe it having moistened a rag, having wrung it out. If ground that was blackened becomes stained, he should wipe it having moistened a rag, having wrung it out. If the ground has not been treated, he should sweep it having sprinkled it all over with water, thinking: Take care lest the dwelling-place is sullied with dust'. Having looked for (any) rubbish, he should remove it to one side..."

We may believe that thinking of concepts concerning the cleaning of our house may hinder the practice of satipaṭṭhāna. We may be inclined to think that while doing chores in our home there cannot be awareness of nāma and rūpa. Both monks and laypeople have to perform tasks in their daily lives and they have to pay attention to concepts, but there can be awareness and understanding of thinking as a conditioned nāma and there can also be awareness of other realities which appear. Seeing and visible object appear time and again and in being aware of their characteristics they can be known as they are. The Buddha exhorted the monks very often to be aware during all their activities and even when this was not always expressively mentioned, it was understood. When we read about the monks chores we can be reminded to be aware, also while we are doing such tasks, just as the monks.

A suitable climate is a natural decisive support-condition for the development of paññā. We read in the Commentary to the "Satipaṭṭhāna Sutta", the "Papañcasūdanī"[3], in the Introduction, about the reason why the Buddha preached this sutta to the people of the Kurus:

> "The inhabitants of the Kuru country- bhikkhus, bhikkhunīs, upāsakas, upāsikās (layfollowers)- by reason of their country being blessed with a perfect climate and through their enjoyment of other comfortable conditions were always healthy in body and in mind. They, happy with healthy minds and bodies, and having the power of knowledge, were capable of receiving deep teachings. . ."

A suitable climate and other favorable circumstances were not the only conditions for the people of Kuru to receive the teachings. They must have listened to the Dhamma and accumulated understanding in the past.

Oppressive weather and bad food can be a natural decisive support-condition for dosa which may be so strong that it leads to killing or the performing of other evil deeds. Habits such as going to sleep and waking up at a particular time come to us naturally, they are conditioned by way of natural decisive support. If we are not negligent, sati can arise before going to sleep and also as soon as we wake up. Someone who is indolent is bound to have attachment before he goes to sleep and when he wakes up. We may regret that there is not often sati before going to sleep and when we wake up, but when we have more understanding of conditions we see that sati is anattā, that it cannot arise at will.

The place where someone is born and where he lives can be a natural decisive support-condition for paññā. Birth in the human plane and in a place where we can hear the Dhamma is rare. By the following sutta we can be reminded not to waste any opportunity to develop right understanding. We read in the "Gradual Sayings" (I, Book of the Ones, Ch XIX, Trifling):

> "Even as, monks, in this Rose-apple Land trifling in number are the pleasant parks, the pleasant groves, the pleasant grounds and lakes, while more numerous are the steep precipitous places, unfordable rivers, dense thickets of stakes and thorns, and inaccessible mountains,- just so few in number are those beings that are born on land: more numerous are the beings that are born in water.

---

[3] Middle Length Sayings I, no. 10. The Sutta and Commentary are translated by Ven. Soma, in "The Way of Mindfulness", B.P.S. Kandy.

Just so few in number are the beings that are reborn among men: more numerous are the beings that are born among others than men.

Just so few in number are those beings that are reborn in the middle districts: more numerous are those reborn in the outlying districts, among the undiscerning barbarians.

Just so few in number are those beings that are wise, quick-witted, not deaf or dumb, competent to judge the meaning of what is spoken well or ill: more numerous are those beings that are foolish, slow-witted, deaf or dumb, incompetent to judge the meaning of what is spoken well or ill.

Just so few in number are those beings that are possessed of the ariyan eye of wisdom[4]: more numerous are those sunk in ignorance and bewilderment.

Just so few in number are those beings that get the chance of seeing a Tathāgata[5]: more numerous are they that do not.

Just so few in number are those beings that welcome, when they hear it, the Dhamma and Discipline set forth by a Tathāgata: more numerous are they that do not.

Just so few in number are those beings, that, on hearing Dhamma, learn it by heart: more numerous are they that do not.

Just so few in number are those beings that examine the meaning of the doctrines they have learnt by heart... that, understanding the meaning and understanding the doctrine, live in accordance with it... that are stirred by stirring topics... that, being stirred, strive systematically... that, making resolution their object, win concentration, win one-pointedness of mind... that gain the best of food and condiments: more numerous are they that do not, but just exist on gathered scraps and food collected in a bowl.

Just so few in number are those beings that are winners of the essence of the meaning, the essence of Dhamma, the essence of release: more numerous are those that do not.

Wherefore I say to you, monks, thus must you train yourselves: We will become winners of the essence of the meaning, of the essence of Dhamma, of the essence of release. That is how you must train yourselves."

---

[4] The path, with insight.

[5] The "Thus-gone", epithet of the Buddha.

10 Prenascence, Postnascence-Condition

Phenomena can condition other phenomena by way of conascence (sahajāta-paccaya), by way of prenascence (purejāta-paccaya) or by way of postnascence (pacchajāta-paccaya). In the case of conascence-condition, a conditioning phenomenon (paccaya dhamma) arises together with the phenomenon it conditions (paccayupanna dhamma). In the case of prenascence-condition, a phenomenon has arisen prior to the phenomenon it conditions. In the case of postnascence-condition, a phenomenon conditions another phenomenon which has arisen prior to itself and has not fallen away yet.

As to prenascence-condition, this is twofold: base-prenascence-condition and object-prenascence-condition.

The rūpas which are bases (vatthus) condition the cittas which are dependent on them by way of prenascence, purejāta-paccaya. As we have seen (in Ch 6), the rūpas which are the sense-bases condition the cittas which are dependent on those bases by way of dependence-condition, nissaya-paccaya. These realities, the rūpas which are bases and the cittas which are dependent on them, are the same as in the case of prenascence-dependence-condition. However, they are treated separately under prenascence-condition with the purpose of showing that the conditioning realities have arisen prior to the conditioned realities.

Seeing arises at the eye-base (cakkhu-vatthu). This rūpa which is the eye-sense (cakkhu pasāda-rūpa) and which has the capacity to receive visible object, is produced by kamma. Rūpa cannot function as base at its arising moment, since it is then too weak. It can only function as base after its arising moment, thus at the time when it is present. It cannot be base either at its dissolution moment. Rūpa lasts longer than citta. When we compare its duration with the duration of citta, rūpa lasts as long as seventeen moments of citta[1]. Thus, the rūpa which can function as eye-base has to arise before seeing-consciousness, and when seeing-consciousness arises it is still present. Kamma keeps on producing this rūpa throughout our life, also when seeing does not arise. It produces all the rūpas which can function as base throughout life, there never is any lack of them.

The eye-base (cakkhu-vatthu) is base only for seeing-consciousness, it is not base for the other cittas arising in the eye-door process; these have the heart-base (hadaya-vatthu) as their base. The previously arisen ear-base conditions hearing-consciousness, thus, it conditions it by way of prenascence-condition. The other sense-bases also condition the cittas which are dependent on them after having

---

[1] See Appendix 1 where it is explained that a sense object which is rūpa and which is experienced by several cittas arising in a sense-door process lasts as long as seventeen moments of citta. When we are more precise, we can divide one moment of citta into three extremely short periods: its arising moment (uppāda khaṇa), the moment of its presence (tiṭṭhi khaṇa) and its dissolution moment (bhaṅga khaṇa). When we take these three periods of citta into consideration, the duration of rūpa is, compared to the duration of citta, three times seventeen, thus, fiftyone moments. Rūpa has after its arising moment fortynine moments of presence and then there is its dissolution moment.

previously arisen, thus by way of prenascence-condition. We read in the "Paṭṭhāna" (II, Analytical Exposition of the Conditions, 10, Prenascence-Condition):

> "Eye-base is related to eye-consciousness element and its associated states[2] by prenascence-condition.
>
> Ear-base is related to ear-consciousness element and its associated states by prenascence-condition.
>
> Nose-base is related to nose-consciousness element and its associated states by prenascence-condition.
>
> Tongue-base is related to tongue-consciousness element and its associated states by prenascence-condition.
>
> Body-base is related to body-consciousness element and its associated states by prenascence-condition."

It seems that seeing, hearing or thinking occur all at the same time, but they arise at different moments, they are dependent on different bases and they experience different objects. When we study the manifold conditions for the realities which arise it will be clearer that there is no self who coordinates all the different experiences. The above quoted text reminds us that seeing, hearing and the other sense-cognitions are only elements, not self. In being mindful of one reality at a time, visible object, sound and the other sense objects can be clearly distinguished from each other. It will be more clearly understood that eye-sense is different from ear-sense and the other senses. As right understanding develops we shall be less inclined to confuse the different realities and to take them for a "whole", for a person.

The heart-base is the base for all the cittas other than the five pairs of sense-cognitions (seeing, hearing, etc., which are either kusala vipāka or akusala vipāka), and it conditions them by way of prenascence-condition. Only at the moment of rebirth the heart-base conditions the paṭisandhi-citta by way of conascence-condition, sahajāta paccaya. At that moment kamma produces the paṭisandhi-citta and the heart-base simultaneously (see Ch 5). We read in the "Paṭṭhāna (same section as the above quoted text, XII) where the heart-base is referred to as "this matter" :

> "Depending on this matter, mind-element and mind-consciousness- element arise; that matter is related to mind-element and its associated states by prenascence-condition; is sometimes related to mind-consciousness-element and its associated states by prenascence-condition, and is sometimes not related by prenascence-condition."

Mind-element, mano-dhātu, includes the pañca-dvārāvajjana-citta, five-sense-door adverting-consciousness, and the two types of sampaṭicchana-citta, receiving-consciousness, which are kusala vipāka and akusala vipāka. Mind-consciousness-element, mano-viññāṇa-dhātu, includes the cittas other than the dvi-pañca-viññāṇas (two pairs of sense-cognitions) and the cittas classified as mind-element. Thus, the mind-consciousness element which is not conditioned by heart-base by way of prenascence, as referred to in the text, is the paṭisandhi-citta. This citta is conditioned by heart-base by way of conascence.

---

[2] The associated dhammas are the accompanying cetasikas.

It is of no use to speculate where the heart-base is, but we should know that cittas do not arise outside the body. In the planes of existence where there are five khandhas, that is to say, nāma and rūpa, each citta needs a physical base or place of origin, and these are the five sense-bases and the heart-base. This reminds us of the interdependence of nāma and rūpa from birth to death.

As regards object-prenascence-condition, ārammaṇa-purejāta-paccaya, this refers to rūpa which can be object of citta. Since rūpa is weak at its arising moment, it can only be experienced by citta during the moments of its presence. Thus, rūpa which is object of citta has arisen previously to that citta; it conditions that citta by way of prenascence. Visible object which impinges on the eyesense is not experienced immediately; there are first bhavanga-cittas[3], and then the eye-door adverting-consciousness arises which is the first citta of the eye-door process which experiences visible object. This citta arises at the heart-base which has previously arisen and which conditions the citta by way of base-prenascence-condition. It is succeeded by seeing-consciousness which arises at the eye-base and then by other cittas of the eye-door process which arise at the heart-base. Both base and sense object condition the cittas by way of prenascence. It is the same for the cittas which experience sense-objects through the other sense-doors[4]. We read in the "Paṭṭhāna" (Analytical Exposition, same section as quoted above) about the object-prenascence-condition. Visible object is here referred to as "visible object-base", and the same for the other sense objects. The text states:

> "Visible object-base is related to eye-consciousness element and its associated states by prenascence-condition.
>
> Sound-base is related to ear-consciousness element and its associated states by prenascence-condition.
>
> Odour-base is related to nose-consciousness element and its associated states by prenascence-condition.
>
> Taste-base is related to tongue-consciousness element and its associated states by prenascence-condition.
>
> Tangible object-base is related to body-consciousness element and its associated states by prenascence-condition.
>
> Visible object-base, sound-base, odour-base, taste-base, tangible object-base is related to mind-element and its associated states by prenascence-condition."

---

[3] Life-continuum. The bhavanga-cittas experience the same object as the paṭisandhi-citta. They do not experience the objects which impinge time and again on the six doors.

[4] Rūpa does not condition nāma by way of prenascence-condition in the four arūpa-brahma planes since there is no rūpa in those planes. Birth in the arūpa-brahma planes is the result of arūpa-jhāna. Those who see the disadvantage of rūpa cultivate arūpa-jhāna. Neither does prenascence-condition occur in the asaññā-satta plane, the plane of non-percipient beings, where there is no nāma. Birth in that plane is the result of rūpa-jhāna.

By the development of satipaṭṭhāna we can prove that our life consists of nāma and rūpa arising because of conditions. Nāma experiences an object and rūpa does not know anything. When seeing appears there can be awareness of its characteristic so that it can be understood as a reality, an element which experiences visible object through the eye-door. When awareness arises of the reality which appears through the eyedoor, it can be understood as an element which does not know anything, which does not see, feel or remember. Realities appear through the six doors time and again and when right understanding develops, nāma can be known as nāma and rūpa as rūpa, and in this way their different characteristics will be distinguished. When we are eating there is flavour and tasting, when we touch something there is tangible object and body-consciousness. When these realities appear and awareness arises there is no need to think of sense-bases, sense objects or any other terms we have learnt from the texts. In being mindful of the characteristics of realities as they appear one at a time, we shall be able to verify the truth that all phenomena which appear are dhammas devoid of self.

We read in the "Kindred Sayings" (IV, Saḷāyatana-vagga, Part I, First Fifty, paragraph 1):

> "Thus have I heard: - The Exalted One was once staying near Sāvatthī, at Jeta Grove, in Anāthapiṇḍika's Park. Then the Exalted One addressed the monks, saying: - Monks.'
>
> Lord,' responded those monks to the Exalted One.
>
> The Exalted One spoke thus: - The eye, monks, is impermanent. What is impermanent, that is dukkha. What is dukkha, that is void of the self. What is void of the self, that is not mine; I am not it; it is not my self. That is how it is to be regarded with perfect insight of what it really is.
>
> The ear... the nose... the tongue... the body... the mind is impermanent. What is impermanent, that is dukkha. What is dukkha, that is void of the self. What is void of the self, that is not mine; I am not it; it is not my self. That is how it is to be regarded with perfect insight of what it really is. So seeing, monks, the well-taught ariyan disciple is repelled by eye, ear, nose, tongue, body, and mind. Being repelled by them, he lusts not for them. Not lusting, he is set free. In this freedom comes insight of being free. Thus he realizes: - Rebirth is destroyed, lived is the righteous life, done is the task, for life in these conditions there is no hereafter.' "

We read in the same section (paragraph 4):

> "Visible objects, sounds, scents, savours, things tangible... mind-states (dhammas) are impermanent... what is impermanent, that is dukkha. What is dukkha, that is void of the self. What is void of the self, that is not mine; I am not it; it is not my self. That is how it is to be regarded with perfect insight of what it really is.
>
> So seeing, monks, the well-taught ariyan disciple is repelled by visible objects, by sounds, scents, savours, things tangible. He is repelled by mind-states. Being repelled by them, he lusts not for them. Not lusting, he is set free. In this freedom comes insight of being free. Thus he realizes:

Rebirth is destroyed. Lived is the righteous life, done is the task, for life in these conditions there is no hereafter.' "

Clinging to the belief that persons and things exist and that we can own them causes a great deal of suffering. The "worldly conditions" of gain and loss, honour and dishonour, praise and blame, wellbeing and misery change all the time. Loss, sickness and death can occur quite suddenly; they are beyond control, but we tend to forget the truth. We cannot expect immediately to have less clinging to people and things. Even the sotāpanna, the person who has attained the first stage of enlightenment and who has no more wrong view of self, still has attachment and sadness. Only the arahat has eradicated all kinds of clinging. However, when we read the Tipiṭaka we can appreciate the numerous reminders of the truth that there is no person, only different elements which are devoid of self. These texts remind us of the truth and they can give us confidence to begin to develop the Path in order to see the realities of our life as elements which arise because of their appropriate conditions and are beyond control.

As to postnascence-condition, pacchajāta-paccaya, citta and its accompanying cetasikas support the rūpas of the body which have arisen previously and have not fallen away yet. Thus, in this way citta conditions these rūpas by way of postnascence-condition. Citta does not cause the arising of the rūpas it conditions by way of postnascence, these rūpas have arisen already prior to the citta; it supports and consolidates these rūpas which are still present, since rūpa lasts as long as seventeen moments of citta.

Citta is postnascence-condition for the previously arisen rūpas of the body which have been produced by the four factors of kamma, citta, temperature and nutrition and which have not fallen away yet. Citta supports and consolidates these rūpas. The paṭisandhi-citta cannot be postnascence-condition, since there is no previously arisen rūpa at the first moment of life. At the first moment of life kamma produces rūpas simultaneously with the paṭisandhi-citta, but after that, throughout our life, citta is postnascence-condition for the previously arisen rūpas of the body. The five pairs of sense-cognitions do not produce rūpa, but they condition the previously arisen rūpas of the body by way of postnascence, they consolidate these[5]. The arūpāvara vipākacittas[6] which arise in the arūpa-brahma planes cannot be postnascence-condition, since there is no rūpa in those planes.

In the case of base and object which are prenascence-condition, rūpa conditions nāma, whereas in the case of postnascence-condition nāma conditions rūpa. The teaching of prenascence-condition, purejāta-paccaya, conascence-condition, sahajāta-paccaya, and postnascence-condition, pacchajāta-paccaya, reminds us of the intricacy of the relationship between different phenomena. Seeing, for example, is the result of kamma and it is dependent on the previously arisen eye-base which is

---

[5] The cittas which produce rūpa condition their arising by way of conascence-condition and dependence-condition, see Ch 5 and 6. As explained, the five sense-cognitions of seeing, hearing, etc., do not produce rūpas, but they consolidate the rūpas which have been produced before by one of the four factors.

[6] These cittas are the results of arūpa-jhāna and they perform the function of rebirth and of bhavanga.

also produced by kamma. Seeing experiences visible object which has previously arisen but which does not last longer than seventeen moments of citta. There is no self who could arrange for seeing to find its proper base; the eye-base has previously arisen and is already there when seeing arises. There is no self who could fetch visible object at the right moment so that seeing can see it and the other cittas of the eye-door process can also experience it, before it falls away. Visible object arises together in a group of rūpas including the four Great Elements and these condition it by way of dependence-condition, nissaya-paccaya, and by conascence-condition, sahajāta-paccaya, but seeing does not experience the other rūpas which arise together with visible object; it only sees visible object, that is, what appears through eyesense. Several conditions coincide and this makes it possible for seeing to arise at the eye-base and to see visible object. We take the experiences which occur time and again in our daily life for granted, but they all are dependent on several conditions, they are interrelated in different ways. Cittas and the rūpas of the body are interrelated, they need one another. Seeing and all other cittas support and consolidate the rūpas of the body which have already arisen, they condition them by way of post-nascence. The different conditions for the phenomena of our life are operating right at this moment.

Shortly before death kamma does not produce the heart-base anymore. The cittas arising shortly before death are depending on one last heart-base and this ceases with the ceasing of the dying-consciousness. At the simultaneous arising of the heart-base and citta, birth occurs and at the simultaneous ceasing of the heart-base and citta, death occurs. The dying-consciousness produces rūpa (except in the case of the arahat) and these rūpas last only seventeen moments of citta. At death, also nutrition ceases to produce rūpa and only temperature, which produces rūpas both in the body and in dead matter, keeps on producing rūpas of the corpse that is left. All this reminds us of the frailty of life which consists of only nāma and rūpa depending on conditions.

11 Repetition-Condition

Repetition-condition, āsevana-paccaya, pertains only to nāma, namely to the javana-cittas arising in a process of cittas. Javana-cittas are kusala, akusala or, in the case of arahats, kiriya. With regard to cittas of the sense-sphere, kāmāvacara cittas, there are usually seven javana-cittas in a process of cittas and these are all of the same jāti, kusala, akusala or kiriya[1]. The first javana-citta conditions the second javana-citta by repetition-condition, āsevana-paccaya, thus, the first javana-citta is the conditioning dhamma (paccaya dhamma) and the second one is the conditioned dhamma (paccayupanna dhamma). After that the second javana-citta which is in its turn the conditioning dhamma, conditions the third one, and so on, until the seventh javana-citta which does not condition the succeeding citta in this way since it is the last javana-citta.

We read in the "Paṭṭhāna (Analytical Exposition, Repetition-condition):

> "Preceding faultless states (kusala dhammas) are related to subsequent faultless states by repetition-condition.
>
> Preceding faulty states (akusala dhammas) are related to subsequent faulty states by repetition-condition.
>
> Preceding functional indeterminate states[2] are related to subsequent functional indeterminate states by repetition-condition."

We read in the "Visuddhimagga" (XVII, 87) about repetition-condition:

> "A dhamma that assists the efficiency and power of the proximate (next) in the sense of repetition-condition, like repeated application to books, and so on..."

Just as one, in learning by heart, through constant repetition, becomes more proficient in reciting texts, evenso the preceding javana-citta supports the succeeding one by repetition-condition.

In the sense-door process the javana-cittas follow upon the determining-consciousness (votthapana-citta) and in the mind-door process upon the mind-door adverting-consciousness (mano-dvārāvajjana-citta). The citta that performs the function of votthapana, determining, is the ahetuka kiriyacitta classified as mano-dvārāvajjana-citta. The mano-dvārāvajjana-citta performs two functions: in the mind-door process it performs the function of adverting to the object through the mind-door, and in the sense-door process it performs the function of determining and then it is called after its function determining-consciousness, votthapana-citta.

The javana-cittas experience the same object as the preceding cittas in the process, they "run through" the object[3], but, except in the case of the arahat, they experience it in a wholesome way or in an unwholesome way. Whether the javana-cittas are kusala cittas or akusala cittas depends on natural decisive support-condition which includes one's accumulated inclinations, and also on root-condition

[1] Cittas can be of four jātis, or classes, namely: kusala, akusala, vipāka and kiriya. Jāti literally means "birth" or nature.

[2] avyakata dhammas, neither kusala nor akusala, which are in this case functional, kiriya.

[3] Javana can be translated as "running", impulse.

and on several other conditions. When we experience a pleasant object through one of the senses, there may be wise attention or unwise attention to the object. When the determining-consciousness in a sense-door process or the mind-door adverting-consciousness in a mind-door process is followed by kusala javana-cittas there is wise attention, and when they are followed by akusala javana-cittas there is unwise attention.

We have accumulated a great deal of attachment and therefore, lobha-mūla-cittas tend to arise on account of a pleasant object. When, for instance, the first javana-citta is lobha-mūla-citta without wrong view and accompanied by pleasant feeling[4], the succeeding javana-citta which is conditioned by the preceding one by way of repetition-condition, is of the same type and so it is with the following ones. During these moments we accumulate more lobha. When the first javana-citta is kusala citta with paññā, the following javana-cittas are of the same type. During these moments paññā is accumulated.

As we have seen (in Ch 4), each citta conditions the succeeding citta by way of proximity-condition, anantara-paccaya, and by way of contiguity-condition, samanantara-paccaya. Moreover, a preceding citta can condition a succeeding citta by way of decisive support of proximity, anantārupanissaya-paccaya (see Ch 7). Javana-citta, besides being a condition for the next one by way of repetition, is also a condition for the next one by way of proximity, contiguity and decisive support of proximity. Realities can be related to each other by way of several conditions. Repetition-condition only refers to javana-cittas. The last javana-citta in a process does not condition the next citta by way of repetition-condition, because it is succeeded by a citta of a different jāti[5]. The cittas which are conditioned by way of repetition-condition have to be of the same jāti as the conditioning citta. Thus, if the first javana-citta is akusala, the following ones are also akusala, and if the first javana-citta is kusala, the following ones are also kusala.

The following javana-cittas are repetition-condition for the succeeding javana-citta: akusala cittas, mahā-kusala cittas (of the sense-sphere), mahā-kiriyacittas (of the arahat), the smile-producing cittas of the arahat (ahetuka kiriyacitta), the rūpāvacara kusala cittas and kiriyacittas (rūpa-jhānacittas) and the arūpāvacara kusala cittas and kiriyacittas (arūpa-jhānacittas)[6].

The performing of akusala kamma or kusala kamma occurs during the moments of javana and these can produce results later on. Moreover, during the moments of javana unwholesome or wholesome tendencies are being accumulated. Thus, the moments of javana condition our life in the future. When we are not intent on kusala, the javana-cittas are akusala. When we are daydreaming or walking around, there are bound to be akusala cittas but we may not notice this. When we speak, we may not lie or use harsh words, but we may not notice how often we are engaged in idle, useless speech. When we, for example, talk about the weather

---

[4] There are eight types of lobha-mūla-citta, see Appendix 2.

[5] It may be succeeded by tadārammaṇa-citta, registering-consciousness, which is vipākacitta produced by kamma and which still experiences the same object. Or it may be followed by bhavanga-citta, life-continuum.

[6] For details see Appendix 3.

or about what we are going to do tomorrow, we may not notice the many akusala cittas which motivate our speech. Because of natural decisive support-condition one kind of akusala can lead to another kind, and therefore, each kind of akusala is dangerous. So long as we are not an arahat we still have conditions for useless speech, but the study of the Dhamma can remind us to be aware while we speak. By right understanding it can be known whether akusala citta or kusala citta motivates our speech.

When we perform good deeds or evil deeds, javana-cittas arise in many different processes of cittas and each of these javana-cittas conditions the next one by way of repetition-condition, except the seventh javana-citta. The teaching of repetition-condition reminds us of the danger of akusala citta. Not only one akusala citta arises within a process of cittas, but seven similar types of citta arise, succeeding one another, and during these moments we accumulate the tendency to akusala so that akusala citta will arise again in the future. When we see the disadvantage of akusala there are conditions for the arising of kusala citta. Not only one kusala citta arises within a process of citta, but seven similar types of citta arise, succeeding one another. When we apply ourselves to kusala, kusala is being accumulated. This should encourage us to perform all kinds of kusala because this is a condition for the arising again of kusala citta in the future. Even when we speak a word of kindness or help someone just for a moment, for example getting something he needs and handing it to him, there are opportunities for kusala cittas. We should not neglect such opportunities or find them insignificant. Each moment of kusala is valuable because at such a moment we do not think of ourselves, there is no lobha, dosa or moha. A wholesome deed is never lost, even if it seems to be of no importance, because kusala is accumulated and it can be a natural decisive support-condition for kusala in the future.

We read in the "Atthasālinī" (Expositor I, Part IV, Ch VIII, 159, in the section on the bases of meritorious action) that, when one performs dāna, there can be kusala cittas before, during and after the wholesome deed:

> "Now, as to these bases, when we think, I will give in charity', the citta works by one or other of those eight classes of kusala citta of the sense-sphere; in making the gift, we give by one of them; in reflecting, I have given in charity', we reflect by one of them..."

The same is said about the other ways of kusala. It is beneficial to know that there are opportunities for kusala citta, not only at the moments we perform a deed of generosity, but also before and afterwards, while we consider our wholesome deed. However, it depends on conditions at which moment kusala citta arises; it is not in anyone's power to make kusala citta arise at will. It may happen that after having given a gift we have regret and then there are akusala cittas. We should not have aversion towards akusala citta which arises, because then we accumulate more akusala. Akusala citta arises because of conditions. Akusala can be the object of mindfulness, so that it can be seen as non-self. At the moment of mindfulness there is kusala citta.

Kusala javana-cittas of the sense sphere, mahā-kusala cittas, are classified as eight types:

- Accompanied by pleasant feeling, with wisdom, unprompted,
- Accompanied by pleasant feeling, with wisdom, prompted,
- Accompanied by pleasant feeling, without wisdom, unprompted,
- Accompanied by pleasant feeling, without wisdom, prompted,
- Accompanied by indifferent feeling, with wisdom, unprompted,
- Accompanied by indifferent feeling, with wisdom, prompted,
- Accompanied by indifferent feeling, without wisdom, unprompted,
- Accompanied by indifferent feeling, without wisdom, prompted.

There are different conditioning factors for these eight types of kusala citta; if we have more knowledge of these factors we shall understand more clearly the great diversity of citta. Cittas are variegated because they are conditioned by different roots which have different intensities. The paññā which may accompany citta can be of many degrees and intensities. It can be intellectual understanding which stems from reading and considering, or it can be direct understanding of the characteristics of realities. Citta can be conditioned by the four predominant factors of chanda (desire-to-do), viriya (energy), (firmness of) citta or vimaṃsa (investigation of Dhamma, paññā cetasika)[7] and these can be of many degrees. Citta experiences objects and these can condition citta in different ways: by way of object-condition, of object-predominance-condition or of decisive support of object[8]. Kusala citta is accompanied by different sobhana cetasikas which condition the citta. We all have different accumulations and thus the type of kusala citta and its intensity varies for different people. Although there is a great diversity of kusala cittas, the Buddha, by his omniscience, classified them as eight types.

The "Atthasālinī" (in the same section as quoted above, 160, 161) mentions the eight types of kusala citta and states that the Buddha's knowledge is more infinite than space, the worldsystems, and the beings in the worldsystems. We read:

> "... Now, all these classes of kusala cittas experienced in the realm of sense, arising in the countless beings in the countless world-systems, the Supreme Buddha, as though weighing them in a great balance, or measuring them by putting them in a measure, has classified by means of his omniscience, and has shown them to be eight, making them into eight similar groups..."

The javana-cittas arising in one process of citta are of the same jāti, that is, kusala, akusala or, in the case of arahats, kiriya (inoperative), since the arahat does not accumulate any more kamma. However, the javana-cittas arising in one process of cittas may sometimes be of a different plane of citta. There are four planes of citta: the sensuous plane of consciousness, the plane of rūpa-jhānacitta, of arūpa-jhānacitta and of lokuttara citta. Cittas of the sensuous plane of consciousness, kāmāvacara cittas, experience sense objects. Jhānacittas do not experience sense objects but they experience with absorption one of the meditation subjects of samatha. Lokuttara cittas experience nibbāna.

---

[7] See Ch 3.

[8] See Ch 2, Ch 3 and Ch 7.

When someone develops samatha and is about to attain jhāna, first, in the process of cittas leading to the attainment of jhāna, kāmāvacara cittas arise, which are, in the case of non-arahats, mahā-kusala cittas experiencing the meditation subject through the mind-door[9]. Each one of the mahā-kusala cittas is repetition-condition for the next one and the last mahā-kusala citta in that process conditions the jhāna-citta by way of repetition-condition. The jhāna-citta is also kusala citta but of a higher plane of citta. When someone is not yet skilled, only one moment of jhāna-citta arises, but when he has become proficient many moments of jhānacitta can arise (Visuddhimagga IV, 78, and IV, 125). Each one of these jhānacittas conditions the next one by way of repetition-condition.

In the process of cittas leading to enlightenment, first mahā-kusala cittas[10] arise accompanied by paññā which clearly sees the reality appearing at that moment as impermanent, dukkha or anattā. One of these three characteristics of reality is at that moment penetrated by paññā since citta can experience only one object at a time. Each of these mahā-kusala cittas is repetition-condition for the next one. The last mahā-kusala-citta in that process, arising before the magga-citta conditions the magga-citta by way of repetition-condition[11]. The magga-citta is of a higher plane of citta, it is lokuttara kusala citta. The magga-citta is immediately succeeded by its result, the phala-citta, but it does not condition the phala-citta by way of repetition-condition since the phala-citta is of a different jāti, the jāti which is vipāka. The phala-citta performs the function of javana, but it is not repetition-condition for the succeeding citta.

When we develop vipassanā, awareness of nāma and rūpa occurs during the moments of javana. Each javana-citta conditions the next one by repetition-condition and in this way understanding can be accumulated.

When mindfulness does not arise, the javana-cittas are bound to be accompanied by clinging. When we, for example, use a soft cushion, we are likely to cling but we may not notice it. When sati arises, softness can be understood as only a rūpa, not a cushion, or, when the experience of softness is the object of sati, it can be realized as only a nāma, an experience. We may think that we can possess things and this can lead to covetousness, avarice, jealousy and many other kinds of defilements. In reality there is no possessor, only seeing which experiences visible object, or touching which experiences tangible object, and other moments of citta experiencing one object at a time. All these realities fall way, they do not stay. Gradually we may know the difference between moments without sati, when we cling to concepts we are thinking of, and moments with sati, when only one reality at a time appears through one of the six doors. Not theoretical understanding, but only direct understanding of realities can lead to eradication of defilements.

---

[9] See Appendix 3 for details.

[10] See Appendix 3 for details.

[11] This mahā-kusala citta experiences nibbāna. When it precedes the magga-citta of the sotāpanna it is called change-of-lineage, gotrabhū, and when it precedes the magga-citta of the three higher stages of enlightenment it is called purification, vodāna. See Ch. 2.

Enlightenment can be attained only if right understanding of realities has been developed in the course of countless lives.

The following sutta from the "Kindred Sayings" (V, Mahā-vagga, Book II, XLVI, Kindred Sayings on the Limbs of Wisdom, Ch IV, paragraph 8, Restraint and hindrance) reminds us of the importance of listening to the Dhamma and considering it as condition for the development of the factors leading to enlightenment. We read that the Buddha said:

> "Monks, there are these five checks, hindrances and corruptions of the heart, which weaken insight. What five?
>
> Sensual desire, monks, is a check and hindrance, a corruption of the heart, that weakens insight. Malevolence... sloth and torpor... excitement and flurry... doubt and wavering... These five... weaken insight.
>
> The seven limbs of wisdom[12], monks, if unrestrained, unhindered, if cultivated and made much of with uncorrupted heart, conduce to realizing the fruits of liberation by knowledge. What seven?
>
> Herein a monk cultivates the limb of wisdom that is mindfulness... the limb of wisdom that is investigation of the Dhamma... the limb of wisdom that is energy... the limb of wisdom that is rapture (pīti), the limb of wisdom that is tranquillity... the limb of wisdom that is concentration... the limb of wisdom that is equanimity, that is based on seclusion, on dispassion, on cessation, that ends in self-surrender.
>
> Now, monks, at the time when the ariyan disciple makes the Dhamma his object, gives attention to it, with all his mind considers it, with ready ear listens to the Dhamma, - at such time these five hindrances exist not in him: at such time the seven limbs of wisdom by cultivation go to fulfilment..."

[12] Bojjhangas or factors of enlightenment.

12 Kamma and Vipāka-Condition

The term kamma is generally used for good and bad deeds, but kamma is actually cetanā cetasika, volition. Cetanā arises with each citta and it can therefore be kusala, akusala, vipāka or kiriya. Cetanā directs the associated dhammas and coordinates their tasks (Atthasālinī, Book I, Part IV, Chapter I, 111).

There are two kinds of kamma-condition: conascent kamma-condition and asynchronous kamma-condition. If we remember that kamma is cetanā cetasika and that cetanā arises with each citta we can understand what conascent kamma-condition is. Cetanā which arises with each citta directs the associated dhammas to accomplish their functions; it conditions these dhammas by way of conascent kamma-condition, sahajāta kamma-paccaya.

Cetanā which accompanies kusala citta and akusala citta has a double function: it directs the tasks of the associated dhammas and it has the function of "willing" or activity in good and bad deeds. In this last function it is capable to produce the results of good and bad deeds later on. Kusala cetanā and akusala cetanā that produce the appropriate results of good deeds or bad deeds later on condition these results by way of asynchronous kamma-condition. Thus, this is kamma operating from a different time (nāṇakkhaṇika kamma-paccaya), it is different from conascent kamma-condition.

As regards conascent kamma-condition, sahajāta kamma-paccaya, the cetanās accompanying all eightynine types of citta[1] are conascent kamma-condition for the citta and the other cetasikas they accompany as well as for the rūpa produced by them. The cetanā which accompanies kusala citta and akusala citta conditions citta, the other cetasikas and the rūpa produced by them by way of conascent kamma-condition, sahajāta-kamma-paccaya. Vipākacitta and kiriyacitta can also produce rūpa[2]; the accompanying cetanā conditions citta, the other cetasikas and rūpa by way of conascent- kamma-condition, sahajāta kamma-paccaya. Seeing, hearing and the other sense-cognitions are vipākacittas which do not produce rūpa, but the accompanying cetanā conditions citta and the other cetasikas by way of conascent kamma-condition. When the paṭisandhi-citta arises the accompanying cetanā conditions that citta, the other cetasikas and also the kamma-produced rūpa which arises at the same time by way of conascent kamma-condition (Paṭṭhāna, Faultless Triplet, Investigation Chapter, Kamma, paragraph 427, vii b).

Asynchronous kamma-condition, nāṇakkhaṇika kamma-paccaya[3], pertains to kusala cetanā or akusala cetanā which is able to produce later on results of good or evil deeds committed through body, speech and mind. The cetanā, volition

1 Cittas which are kusala citta, akusala citta, vipākacitta and kiriyacitta. For the classification of the different cittas see my "Abhidhamma in Daily Life", Ch 23.

2 Citta, being one of the four factors which produces groups of rūpas of the body, can produce groups of rūpas consisting of at least the eight "inseparable rūpas" (the four great Elements, colour, odour, flavour and nutritive essense) and in addition there can be other rūpas as well in such a group.

3 Nāṇakkhaṇika literally means: working from a different time and this pertains to the fact that it produces result later on.

or intention, which motivates a good or bad deed falls away, but since each citta conditions the next one in the cycle of birth and death, the force of cetanā is accumulated from moment to moment so that it can produce result later on. It conditions the result in the form of vipākacitta and specific rūpas of the body[4] by way of asynchronous kamma-condition. When one, for example, slanders, there is akusala kamma through speech and this can produce akusala vipāka later on. The akusala cetanā or kamma conditions the vipākacitta which arises later on by way of asynchronous kamma-condition. At the same time, the akusala cetanā is related to the citta and cetasikas it accompanies and to speech intimation (vacīviññatti), a rūpa produced by citta, by way of conascent kamma-condition. Akusala cetanā and kusala cetanā condition other phenomena by way of conascent kamma-condition and also by way of asynchronous kamma-condition.

Kusala kamma and akusala kamma through body, speech and mind can be of different degrees. Kamma is not always a "completed action". There are certain constituent factors which make kamma a completed action. For example, in the case of killing there have to be: a living being, consciousness of there being a living being, intention of killing, effort and consequent death (Atthasālinī, I, Book I, Part III, Ch V, 97). If one of these factors is lacking kamma is not a completed action. Akusala kamma which is a completed action is capable of producing an unhappy rebirth. Not only birth is the result of kamma, but also the experience of pleasant or unpleasant objects through the senses, which are seeing, hearing, smelling, tasting or experiencing tangible objects through the bodysense throughout life are the result of kamma. Some kammas produce their results in the same life in which they were committed, some in the next life, some in later lives.

We read in the "Visuddhimagga" (XIX, 14-17) about different ways of classifying kamma. Kamma can be classified as weighty, habitual, death-threshold and reserve or effective kamma[5] (Visuddhimagga XIX, 15,16). Weighty (garuka) kamma is very unprofitable kamma, such as the killing of a parent, or very profitable kamma, such as jhānacitta. Habitual (āciṇṇa) kamma is what one usually and repeatedly does. Death-threshold (āsanna) kamma is what is vividly remembered just before death. Reserve or effective kamma (kamma kaṭattā, because of being performed) is kamma which produces rebirth if there is no opportunity for one of the three foregoing kammas to do so.

Do we know which type of kamma we usually and repeatedly perform? Is it akusala kamma through body, speech or mind, or is it kusala kamma? When we perform kusala kamma such as generosity do we know whether the kusala citta is accompanied by paññā or unaccompanied by paññā[6] ? The development of

---

[4] Kamma is one of the four factors which produces rūpas of the body. It produces rūpas such as the sense-bases, the heart-base and femininity or masculinity.

[5] Kamma kaṭattā, literally: because of kamma that has been performed. Sometimes it is translated as "stored up kamma", but this is misleading, since it may suggest something which is permanent. Kamma falls away immediately, but its force is accumulated in the citta. Since our life is an unbroken series of cittas arising and falling away, and each citta conditions the next citta, kamma can produce result later on.

[6] See Appendix 2 for the different types of kusala citta.

satipaṭṭhāna, right understanding of nāma and rūpa, is kusala kamma. When we see the benefit of considering nāma and rūpa over and over again, in one's daily life, it can become habitual kamma, often performed. Then paññā can be developed which leads to the end of rebirth-producing kamma.

Kamma can also be classified as: reproductive, consolidating, obstructive and destructive. Reproductive kamma (janaka kamma) produces nāma and rūpa at birth and in the course of life. Consolidating or supportive kamma (upatthambaka kamma) consolidates the result which has been produced by reproductive kamma. Supportive kusala kamma can prolong the arising of pleasant results in the form of health or wealth and supportive akusala kamma can prolong the arising of painful feeling and the experience of other unpleasant objects in the course of life. Obstructive or counteractive kamma (upapīḷaka kamma) weakens, interrupts or retards the result of kusala kamma or akusala kamma. Someone who has a happy rebirth may suffer ill health so that he cannot enjoy pleasant objects. An animal who has an unhappy rebirth may still have a comfortable life because of obstructive kamma. Destructive kamma (upaghātaka kamma) counteracts other weaker kamma to produce its result; instead it produces its own result.

A deed can produce result when the time is right[7]. Some deeds produce result in this life, some in the next life and some after aeons. The lokuttara kusala citta, the magga-citta, produces immediate result in the form of the phalacitta, fruition-consciousness (lokuttara vipākacitta), without any interval. The magga-citta is anantara kamma-paccaya for the phala-citta (anantara means: without interval).

We have accumulated many different kammas and we do not know which of these will produce result at a particular moment; as we have seen (in Ch 8), kamma that produces result is also natural decisive support-condition, pakatūpanissaya paccaya, for that result. Thus, kamma performed in the past is kamma-condition and natural decisive support-condition, that is, a cogent reason for the result it produces.

Only a Buddha has full knowledge of the true nature of kamma and vipāka and this knowledge is not shared by his disciples ("Visuddhimagga" XIX, 17).

We do not know which of our deeds will produce rebirth. We read in the "Greater Analysis of Deeds" (Middle Length Sayings III, 136) that the Buddha, while staying

---

[7] We read in the Commentary to the "Book of Analysis", the "Dispeller of Delusion" (Ch 16, Tathāgata Powers 2, 439-443) about four factors which condition kamma to produce result: destiny, or the place where one is born (gati); substratum, including beauty or ugliness in body (upadhi); the time when one is born (kāla) and the "means" (payoga), including skill in one's occupation, in the performing of one's tasks. These four factors can be favorable (sampatti) or unfavorable (vipatti). If they are favorable, akusala kamma has less opportunity and kusala kamma has more opportunity to produce result and if they are unfavorable, akusala kamma has more opportunity and kusala kamma has less opportunity to produce result. For example, if someone is born in a happy plane, if he has beauty of body, if he is born in a favorable time (kāla), when there is a good king and the country is prosperous, if he is successful in his occupation, in the performing of his tasks (payoga), the ripening of akusala kamma is inhibited and there is opportunity for kusala kamma to give results. If these four factors are unfavorable (vipatti), the opposite is the case: akusala kamma has the opportunity to ripen and the results of kusala kamma are inhibited.

near Rajagaha, in the Bamboo Grove, spoke to Ānanda about deeds and their results. We read about someone who performs evil deeds and is of wrong view, and who has an unhappy rebirth. However, for such a person there is also a possibility of a happy rebirth. We read:

> "... As to this, Ānanda, whatever individual there is who makes onslaught on creatures, takes what has not been given... is of false view and who, at the breaking up of the body after dying arises in a good bourn, a heaven world either a lovely deed to be experienced as happiness was done by him earlier, or a lovely deed to be experienced as happiness was done by him later, or at the time of dying a right view was adopted and firmly held by him; because of this, at the breaking up of the body after dying he arises in a good bourn, a heaven world. If he made onslaught on creatures here, took what had not been given... and was of false view, he undergoes its fruition which arises here and now or in another mode."

We then read about someone who is restrained from evil and is of right view, and who has a happy rebirth. However, even for such a person there may be an unhappy rebirth. We read:

> "... As to this, Ānanda, whatever individual there is who is restrained from making onslaught on creatures, is restrained from taking what has not been given... is of right view and who, at the breaking up of the body after dying, arises in the sorrowful ways, a bad bourn, the Downfall, Niraya Hell either an evil deed to be experienced as anguish was done by him earlier, or an evil deed to be experienced as anguish was done by him later, or at the time of dying a false view was adopted and firmly held by him; because if this... he arises in the sorrowful ways... Niraya Hell. And he who was restrained from making onslaught on creatures... and was of right view undergoes its fruition which arises either here and now or in another mode..."

So long as we perform kamma there are conditions for rebirth and there will be dukkha. Kamma is one of the links in the "Dependent Origination" (Paticca Samuppāda), the chain of conditionally arisen phenomena which cause the continuation of the cycle of birth and death. When all defilements have been eradicated there will be no more rebirth. We read in the "Gradual Sayings" (Book of the Tens, Ch XVII, Jāṇussoṇi, paragraph 8, Due to lust, malice and delusion):

> "Monks, the taking of life is threefold, I declare. It is due to lust, malice and delusion. Taking what is not given... wrong conduct in sexual desires... falsehood... spiteful speech... bitter speech... idle babble... coveting... harmfulness... wrong view, is threefold, I declare. It is due to lust, malice and delusion.
>
> Thus, monks, lust is the coming-to-be of a chain of causal action; so is malice. Delusion, monks, is the coming-to-be of a chain of causal action. By destroying lust, by destroying malice, by destroying delusion comes the breaking up of the chain of causal action."

The arahat can still have vipāka which is conditioned by asynchronous kamma-condition, but from the time he attained arahatship he cannot perform new kamma.

The mahā-kiriyacittas (inoperative cittas of the sense sphere which are sobhana, beautiful) of the arahat do not produce vipāka.

As to vipāka-condition, this concerns phenomena which are conascent, arising at the same time. Citta and its accompanying cetasikas which are vipāka, condition one another in this way. We read in the "Visuddhimagga" (XVII,89) that they assist one another "by effortless quiet". They are merely vipāka, they have no other activity. The nature of vipākacitta is altogether different from the nature of kusala citta and akusala citta which are active in a wholesome way or in an unwholesome way. Vipākacitta and its accompanying cetasikas also condition one another by way of conascence-condition and by way of mutuality-condition.

In the planes of existence where the five khandhas (nāma and rūpa) arise, citta produces rūpa which arises at the same time. The vipākacittas, except the five sense-cognitions, which produce rūpa, condition this rūpa by way of vipāka-condition[8] according to the "Paṭṭhāna" (Faultless Triplet, Investigation Chapter, paragraph 428).

In the planes where the five khandhas arise, kamma produces at the first moment of life the rebirth-consciousness (paṭisandhi-citta) which is vipākacitta, as well as rūpa. The rebirth-consciousness conditions the rūpa that is also produced by kamma at the same time by way of vipāka-condition, according to the "Paṭṭhāna" (same section). They are both results of kamma. The paṭisandhi-citta is the first vipākacitta arising in life. When it is the result of kusala kamma birth occurs in a happy plane and when it is the result of akusala kamma birth occurs in an unhappy plane. Kusala kamma and akusala kamma can be of many different degrees and thus the vipāka they produce can also be of different degrees. When the paṭisandhi-citta is the result of weak kusala kamma, it is ahetuka kusala vipākacitta (unaccompanied by sobhana hetus) and in the case of birth as a human, one is handicapped from the first moment of life. The paṭisandhi-citta can also be mahā-vipāka, accompanied by two or three sobhana hetus[9]. The mahā-vipākacitta is also conditioned by way of hetu-paccaya, root-condition. When the paṭi- sandhi-citta is the result of akusala kamma it is ahetuka akusala vipākacitta, and in that case one has an unhappy rebirth in one of the woeful planes.

Human birth is the result of kusala kamma. Paṭisandhi-cittas are variegated; for instance, in the case of a human being, there can be nine different types of paṭisandhi-citta as I explained in my "Abhidhamma in Daily Life"[10] and these can vary greatly as to their nature and intensity. We see a great difference in bodily features: some people are beautiful, some are not beautiful. There are differences in the sense-faculties such as eyesense and earsense. There are differences in bodily strength, some people are apt to have many illnesses and they are weak, some

---

[8] Bhavanga-citta, receiving-consciousness (sampaṭicchana-citta) or investigation-consciousness (santīraṇa-citta) are for example vipākacittas which produce rūpas. See Appendix 1 for these cittas.

[9] By alobha, non-attachment or generosity and by adosa, non-aversion or kindness, or by paññā as well.

[10] One type is ahetuka kusala vipāka, and eight types are mahā-vipākacittas. See my Abhidhamma in Daily Life Ch 11.

have only few illnesses and they are strong. People are born with different degrees of paññā or without it; they have different capabilities to develop paññā. If the paṭisandi-cittas of people were not so different, there would not be such a variety in the characteristics of different people.

The vipākacitta which is paṭisandhi-citta is succeeded by the vipākacitta which is bhavanga-citta because of proximate-condition, contiguity-condition and proximate decisive support-condition. The bhavanga-citta is the same type of citta as the paṭisandhi-citta. There are countless bhavanga-cittas arising throughout life in between the processes of cittas and all of them are of the same type as the paṭisandhi-citta. They maintain the continuity in the life of a person who is born with particular inclinations and capacities.

Throughout life kamma produces vipākacittas arising in processes of cittas which experience pleasant or unpleasant objects. Seeing, for example, is vipākacitta which experiences a pleasant or unpleasant visible object through the eyesense. It merely sees, it does not know whether the object is pleasant or unpleasant. Citta and the accompanying cetasikas condition one another by way of vipāka-condition, they assist one another in "effortless quiet". The succeeding receiving-consciousness, sampaṭicchana-citta[11] , is also vipākacitta, and this is succeeded by another vipākacitta, the investigating-consciousness, santīraṇa-citta. This is succeeded by the determining-consciousness, the votthapana-citta, which is a kiriyacitta. After that the javana-cittas arise which are, in the case of non-arahats, kusala cittas or akusala cittas. When the object is pleasant, lobha-mūla-cittas are likely to arise and when the object is unpleasant, dosa-mūla-cittas are likely to arise. Cittas arise and fall away succeeding one another very rapidly and so long as paññā has not been developed, we do not realize when there is vipākacitta and when there is kusala citta or akusala citta. When we have an unpleasant experience such as an accident we keep on thinking of the concept of a situation or of an event we consider as "our vipāka" and we may wonder why this had to happen to us. We tend to forget that vipākacitta is only one moment which falls away immediately. Instead of thinking of concepts with aversion we should develop understanding of paramattha dhammas, realities which each have their own characteristic and which appear one at a time.

When we see visible object and we like the object it seems that seeing and liking occur at the same time. We do not realize that there is proximity-condition, anantara-paccaya, because of which each citta is succeeded by the next one, without any interval. Or we do not even realize that there is attachment to the object. We may think that there is seeing while there is in reality already clinging. Without knowing it we continue to accumulate more akusala.

It is important to have right understanding of cause and effect in our life. We like to experience pleasant objects and we may think that we can choose ourselves which objects we wish to experience. We buy beautiful things in order to look at them, we prepare delicious food in order to enjoy pleasant flavours. However, something can happen so that our expectations do not come true. It depends on kamma whether we experience a pleasant object or an unpleasant object at a particular

[11] See Appendix I for the cittas arising in a process.

moment. Kamma produces its appropriate result and when it is time for akusala vipāka it is unavoidable. We never know what will happen at the next moment, but when there is more understanding of cause and effect in our life we can be prepared to face whatever may happen. When right understanding arises of kamma and vipāka, the citta is at that moment kusala citta and there is no opportunity for aversion towards unpleasant experiences. In being mindful of the characteristics of seeing, hearing, thinking and the other realities appearing in daily life, ignorance can gradually decrease. We can learn to distinguish between the moments of vipāka and the moments of kusala citta and akusala citta.

13 Nutriment-Condition

There are four kinds of nutriment which are nutriment-condition, āhāra-paccaya. One kind is physical nutriment and three are mental nutriment. The four kinds of nutriment are:

- physical nutriment
- contact (phassa cetasika)
- volition (manosañcetanā which is cetanā cetasika)
- consciousness (viññāṇa)

In the case of nutriment-condition, āhāra-paccaya, a conditioning dhamma maintains and supports the growth and development of the conditioned dhammas[1].

As regards physical nutriment, this sustains the rūpas of the body. Nutritive essence (ojā) present in food that has been taken permeates the body and then new rūpas can be produced. As we have seen, nutrition is one of the four factors which produces rūpas of the body, the other three being kamma, citta and temperature. Nutritive essence is present in all groups of rūpas; it is one of the eight "inseparable rūpas" present in all materiality, no matter it is the body or materiality outside. Nutritive essence arises together with the four Great Elements of solidity, cohesion, temperature and motion, and also with visible object, flavour and odour. Nutritive essence present in the groups of rūpas of the body cannot produce new rūpas without the support of external nutritive essence in food. For the new being in the mother's womb it is necessary that the mother takes food so that nutritive essence present in food can permeate its body. Then nutritive essence can produce new rūpas and thus it goes on throughout life. The nutritive essence which, because of the support of external nutritive essence, produces new rūpas of the body also supports and maintains the groups of rūpas produced by kamma, citta and temperature.

When nutriment has been taken, the nutritive essence present in the body can produce new groups of rūpas, consisting of the eight inseparable rūpas. Nutritive essence present in such an octad can in its turn produce another group of eight "inseparable rūpas" (an octad). In this way several octads produced by nutrition will arise one after the other, and thus, nutriment which has been taken can be sufficient for some time afterwards (Visuddhimagga XX, 37).

Nutritive essence is present in food, but one cannot eat nutritive essence alone. We need also sufficient substance or solidity, so that we do not go hungry. Edible food made into morsels[2] can be swallowed; it has the function of nourishing.

We cannot live without food, but it is dangerous to cling to it. In order to obtain it, people may commit akusala kamma which is capable of producing akusala vipāka. Someone who is greedy may be reborn as a "peta" (ghost). So long as we cling to food there will be rebirth and this is dukkha. We may recollect the disadvantages

[1] The Commmentary to the "Discourse on Right Understanding" (Middle Length Sayings I, 9), the Papañcasūdanī, gives an explanation of the word āhāra. The condition fetches (āharati) its own fruit, therefore it is called āhāra.

[2] The Pāli word kabaliṇkāro āhāro means "morsel food", food that can be swallowed.

of searching for food, the foulness of nutriment and its digestion, with the purpose of having less clinging to food.

We read in the "Visuddhimagga" (I, 89) that the monk should remember that food is not for intoxication, smartening, embellishment or amusement. It should be taken for the sake of the endurance and continuance of the body, for the ending of discomfort and for the assisting of the life of purity (Visuddhimagga I, 91,92). Just as a sick man uses medicine he should use almsfood, so that he will not be feeling hungry anymore, and he should avoid immoderate eating. Thus he will be healthy and blameless and live in comfort (Visuddhimagga I, 94).

We read in the "Visuddhimagga" (Ch XI, 11, and following), in the section on the "Perception of Repulsiveness in Nutriment", about the disadvantages of having to search for food. The monk has to go in dirty places while he walks with his almsbowl. He does not always receive food or he receives unappetizing food. Also when he takes the food, the process of chewing, swallowing and digesting is disgusting, not to speak of the secretion while it is being digested and of its flowing out again. In the Commentary to the "Satipaṭṭhāna Sutta" (I, 10), the "Papañcasūdanī"[3], we read in the section on Mindfulness of the Body, Clear Comprehension in the Partaking of Food and Drink, that in the process of eating and digesting the food, only elements are performing their functions. There is no self, no person who eats. We read:

> "It is oscillation (vāyodhātu, the element of wind or motion) that does the taking onward, the moving away from side to side; and it is oscillation that bears, turns around, pulverizes, causes the removal of liquidity, and expels.
>
> Extension (paṭhavīdhātu, the element of earth or solidity) also does bearing up, turning around, pulverizing and the removal of liquidity.
>
> Cohesion (āpodhātu, the element of water) moistens and preserves wetness.
>
> Caloricity (tejodhātu, the element of heat) ripens or digests the food that goes in.
>
> Space (ākāsadhātu) becomes the way for the entering of the food..."

We read in the "Kindred Sayings" (II, Kindred Sayings on Cause, Ch VII, the Great Chapter, paragraph 63, Child's Flesh) about parents who were with their child in the jungle. Since there was no food and all three of them would have to die of hunger, they slew their child and ate its flesh, not for pleasure, from indulgence, for physical beauty, attractiveness. They took it in order not to die and to be able to cross the jungle. We then read that the Buddha said to the monks:

> "Even so, monks, I declare should solid food be regarded. When such food is well understood, the passions of the five senses are well understood. When the passions of the five senses are well understood, the fetters do not exist bound by which the ariyan disciple could come again to this world."

---

3 Translated by Ven. Soma in "The Way of Mindfulness", B.P.S. Kandy, Sri Lanka.

The Commentary to this sutta states that the Buddha spoke this discourse because the Order received abundant almsfood and requisites, and the Buddha wanted to exhort the monks to make use of the requisites only after wise reflection.

Physical nutriment conditions the rūpas of the body by way of āhāra-paccaya, nutriment-condition. As we have seen, there are three kinds of mental nutriment which are: contact (phassa), (mental) volition (manosañcetanā) and citta (viññāṇa). Just as physical food supports and maintains the body, so does mental nutriment support and maintain the accompanying dhammas. In the case of mental nutriment, the conditioning dhamma is conascent with the conditioned dhammas. The mental nutriments condition the dhammas which arise together with them and the rūpas produced by citta and cetasikas by way of nutriment-condition. At the moment of rebirth the mental nutriments condition the associated dhammas and the rūpa produced by kamma by way of nutriment-condition (Paṭṭhāna, Faultless Triplet, Ch VII, Investigation Chapter, Nutriment, paragraph 429).

As to the mental nutriment which is contact, phassa, this is a cetasika which contacts the object so that citta and the accompanying cetasikas can experience it[4]. Without contact citta and cetasikas could not experience any object, thus, contact supports them, it is a mental nutriment for them. It accompanies each citta and it conditions citta and the accompanying cetasikas by way of āhāra-paccaya, nutriment-condition. It also conditions rūpa produced by citta and cetasikas by way of nutriment-condition. When bodily painful feeling arises, we know that there is contact, otherwise there could not be the experience of an unpleasant object. This experience does not last. When hearing arises we know that there is another kind of contact; it contacts sound so that hearing can experience it. Through mindfulness of realities as they appear one at a time, one can come to understand that there are different contacts all the time and that the experience of the different objects does not last.

As to the mental nutriment which is volition, manosañcetanā[5], this is cetanā cetasika which accompanies all eightynine types of citta, thus it can be of the jāti which is kusala, akusala, vipāka or kiriya. It coordinates the tasks of the citta and cetasikas it accompanies, and it maintains and supports them; thus, it conditions them by way of nutriment-condition. It also conditions the rūpa produced by citta by way of nutriment-condition. As we have seen, cetanā conditions the associated dhammas also by way of conascent kamma-condition, sahajāta kamma-paccaya (see Ch 11).

As to the mental nutriment which is viññāṇa or citta, this refers to each citta. Citta is the chief in cognizing an object, it is the "leader". Without citta, cetasikas could not arise and experience an object. Thus, citta supports and maintains the accompanying cetasikas, it conditions them by way of nutriment-condition. When citta produces rūpa it also conditions that rūpa by way of nutriment-condition.

---

[4] Phassa is nāma, it is not physical contact.

[5] Mano is mind and cetanā is volition. In the context of āhāra-paccaya the word manosañcetanā, mental volition, is used to denote cetanā cetasika.

Thus, at each moment the three mental nutriments of contact, volition and citta support and maintain the dhammas arising together with them, and the rūpa produced by them, by way of nutriment-condition.

The mental nutriments can be considered according to the method of the Paṭṭhāna and also according to the method of the "Dependent Origination" (Paticca samuppāda), the chain of conditionally arisen phenomena which cause the continuation of the cycle of birth and death[6]. According to the method of the Dependent Origination, contact, cetanā and viññāṇa are considered as nutriments which condition the continuation of life in the cycle of birth and death.

Contact is a link in the Dependent Origination and as such it is the condition for feeling, the following link. Contact contacts an object and feeling experiences the "flavour" of that object. Contact conditions the feeling which arises together with it. Because of contact there is feeling, because of feeling there is craving; because of craving there is clinging and this leads to becoming, and thus there is rebirth. We want to live and we have attachment to sense objects; we are never satisfied, and therefore, there are conditions for life to go on. It is not by mere chance that we experience objects through the six doors; all these experiences can arise because of the concurrence of the appropriate conditions.

We should see the disadvantages of contact. In the above quoted sutta of the "Kindred Sayings", after the explanation of the disadvantages of material food by the simile of "Child's Flesh", the disadvantages and dangers of the three kinds of mental nutriment are explained. In order to illustrate the danger of contact, the Buddha used the simile of a cow which stands with a sore hide leaning against the wall. The creatures who live there bite her. The same happens when she leans against a tree and no matter where she stands she will be bitten. We read:

> "Even so do I declare that the food which is contact should be regarded. When such food is well understood, the three feelings[7] are well understood. When the three feelings are well understood, I declare that there is nothing further which the ariyan disciple has to do."

Feeling is rooted in contact and associated with it. We cling to all sense objects and to pleasant feeling arising on account of them, but we should remember the danger of contact which leads to dukkha. The Commentary explains that the bhikkhu who sees the danger of being eaten by the defilement-creatures rooted in the nutriment-contact, becomes detached from contact[8].

The mental nutriment which is volition, cetanā, is also a link in the Dependent Origination. Under this aspect it is cetanā (saṅkhāra or kamma-formations) which is kusala kamma, akusala kamma or "imperturbable" kamma (āneñja, arūpāvacara

---

[6] Twelve factors are links in the chain of the Dependent Origination, and each one conditions the following one. They are: ignorance, kamma-formations (saṅkhāra, rebirth producing volitions), consciousness (viññāṇa), nāma and rūpa, the six bases, contact, feeling, craving, clinging, becoming, birth, old age and death. See "Visuddhimagga" XVII, 101-314.

[7] Pleasant feeling, unpleasant feeling and indifferent feeling.

[8] For the explanations of the three mental nutriments by the Commentary, I used the Notes of Venerable Bodhi in his translation of the Saṁyutta Nikāya.

kusala kamma), and these kammas produce rebirth. In the above quoted sutta we read about a simile of a glowing charcoal-pit to which someone is dragged by two strong men. He wishes to be far from it because if he falls on that heap of charcoal he will have mortal pain and he will die. The Commentary explains that the accumulation of kusala kamma and akusala kamma are like these two strong men, and that his accumulated kamma drags him along to rebirth. The round of birth and death is like the glowing charcoal-pit according to the Commentary. We should see the danger of cetanā which produces rebirth. We read:

> "Even so, monks, I declare that the food which is manosañcetanā (mental volition) should be regarded. When that food is well understood, the three cravings[9] are well understood. When these are well understood, I declare that there is nothing further that the ariyan disciple has to do."

When viññāṇa (consciousness), the third mental nutriment, is considered under the aspect of the Dependent Origination, it is vipākacitta which arises at rebirth and also in the course of life. As a link of the Dependent Origination it is conditioned by saṅkhāra, kamma-formations. Kamma produces the vipākacitta which is the paṭisandhi-citta as well as the vipākacittas arising throughout our life. We read in the above quoted sutta about the simile of a robber who is punished by the King. The King lets him be smitten with hundred spears in the morning, hundred at noon and hundred in the evening. Acording to the Commentary, the King represents kamma, the robber represents the worldling, the threehundred spears represent rebirth-consciousness. The pain from being struck by the spears is like the resultant suffering in the course of life when rebirth has occurred. The nutriment which is consciousness should be regarded as sorrowful as the pain suffered by that robber. We read:

> "Even so, monks, do I declare that the food called consciousness should be regarded. When consciousness, monks, is well understood, nāma and rūpa[10] are well understood. When nāma and rūpa are well understood, I declare that there is nothing further that the ariyan disciple has to do."

When we consider the three kinds of mental nutriment under the aspect of the Dependent Origination, they remind us of the danger of being in the cycle of birth and death. At each moment citta experiences an object, but so long as we cling to the experiencing of objects we cannot see the disadvantages of nutriment. We may not understand, for example, the danger of seeing. Seeing merely experiences visible object and it does not know whether the object is pleasant or unpleasant; at that moment there is no like or dislike. After the seeing, however, there are javana-cittas, and when we are not intent on what is wholesome the javana-cittas are akusala cittas. Most of the time they are akusala cittas. As soon as we have seen food lobha-mūla-cittas tend to arise. The attachment may not be accompanied by pleasant feeling but by indifferent feeling and then we may not know that there is attachment. Akusala cittas arise when we perform unwholesome deeds through the body or through speech, and they may also arise when we do not perform

[9] Craving for sense pleasures, craving for becoming and craving for non-becoming. Craving is the root of mano-sañcetanā according to the Commentary.

[10] In the Dependent Origination consciousness is a link which conditions nāma and rūpa.

such deeds. Countless moments of thinking which are akusala arise in a day, but we usually do not realize that. On account of the objects which are experienced through the senses, defilements arise and they are accumulated from life to life. When we understand the danger of defilements we can be reminded to be aware of the realities which appear. If there is no awareness of akusala, it can never be eradicated.

14 Faculty-Condition

The Pāli term for faculty is "indriya", meaning strength, governing or controlling principle. Indriyas are "leaders" for the associated dhammas; they are leaders each in their own field. In the case of indriya-paccaya, faculty-condition, the conditioning dhamma (paccaya dhamma) has leadership, great control, over the conditioned dhammas (paccayupanna dhammas). Some indriyas are rūpa and some are nāma. We read in the "Visuddhimagga" (XVI, 1) that there are twentytwo indriyas. They are:

- The five senses: the faculties of eye, ear, nose, tongue and body-sense
- mind faculty
- femininity faculty
- masculinity faculty
- life faculty (one is rūpa and one is nāma)
- bodily pleasure faculty
- pain faculty
- pleasant feeling faculty
- unpleasant feeling faculty
- equanimity (indifferent feeling) faculty
- faith faculty
- energy faculty
- mindfulness faculty
- concentration faculty
- understanding faculty
- "I-shall-come-to-know-the-unknown" faculty (anaññātaññassāmī't'indriya)
- higher knowledge faculty (aññindriya)
- faculty of him who knows (aññātāvindriya)

Of these twentytwo faculties, twenty are faculty-condition and two, namely the femininity faculty and the masculinity faculty, are not faculty-condition as we shall see.

The rūpas which are the five sense-bases control the functions of the sense-cognitions (seeing, hearing, etc.), they condition these vipākacittas by way of faculty-condition. They arise previously to the sense-cognitions because rūpa at its arising moment is too weak to be a base for citta. Since rūpa lasts longer than citta, the sense-bases are still present when the sense-cognitions arise and they condition them by way of faculty-condition. They are base-prenascent faculties. Without the eye faculty there cannot be seeing, it conditions seeing-consciousness and its accompanying cetasikas by way of faculty-condition. The rūpa (pasāda-rūpa) which is eyesense is the eye faculty; it is leader in its own field, in seeing. It cannot be leader in the field of hearing.

We read in the "Paṭṭhāna" (Faultless Triplet, VII, Investigation Chapter, paragraph 430) that the faculties which are the five senses are related to the sense-cognitions by way of faculty-condition:

> "Eye-faculty is related to eye-consciousness by faculty-condition; ear-faculty to ear-consciousness... nose-faculty to nose-consciousness... tongue-faculty to tongue-consciousness... body-faculty is related to body-consciousness by faculty-condition."

The rūpas which are the five sense-bases condition the five pairs of sense-cognitions, the dvi-pañca-viññāṇas, also by dependence-condition, nissaya-paccaya (see Ch 6), and by prenascence-condition, pure-jāta-paccaya (see Ch 9), since they have to arise previously to the citta for which they are the base. The faculties which are the senses are kamma-produced rūpas. The quality of these faculties is different for different people: some have keen eyesense, others have weak eyesense, and the same for the other senses.

One may wonder why the rūpas which are the five senses are faculties and why, for example, the four Great Elements on which the other rūpas depend are not faculties. If there were no senses the four Great Elements could not even appear. Objects can only be experienced because there are faculties which condition the experience of objects by way of faculty-condition. When satipaṭṭhāna is not being developed, we cannot really understand the functions of the faculties which are the five senses, we shall have only theoretical understanding of the faculties. Without awareness of realities as they appear one at a time, we do not know when there is seeing and when hearing. Different experiences seem to occur at the same time. In being aware of visible object, the reality which appears through the eyesense, we can begin to understand that visible object could not appear without eyesense; and thus the function of the eye faculty, the "leader" in the field of seeing, will be clearer.

Eyesense is different from earsense or bodysense. The senses do not belong to a self who can coordinate the different functions of seeing, hearing and the other experiences. We are inclined to confuse the different realities which appear at different moments and we cling to a "whole" of impressions.

The "Book of Analysis" (Ch 5, Analysis of the Controlling Faculties, paragraph 220) reminds us that the faculties are non-self. We read:

> "Therein what is controlling faculty of eye? That eye which, derived from the four great essentials (the four great Elements[1]), is sensitive surface... this is an empty village. This is called controlling faculty of eye."

The same is said of the other senses, they all are empty villages. The "Atthasalinī" (II, Book II, Ch III, 309) explains "empty village":

> " And this is an empty village', refers to its being common to many and to the absence of a possessor."

---

[1] The eyesense arises in a group of rūpas which includes the four great Elements of solidity, cohesion, temperature and motion which are present in each group of rūpas. All rūpas other than the four great Elements are "derived rūpas", upādā-rūpas and these are dependent on the four great Elements.There cannot be eyesense without solidity, cohesion, temperature and motion.

Just as an empty village is unoccupied, so the eye and the other senses have no possessor, they are anattā, non-self.

The five faculties which are the five senses (pasāda rūpas) are sense-doors as well as physical bases (vatthus). The heart-base (hadaya-vatthu) is the rūpa which is the physical base for the cittas other than the sense-cognitions. One may wonder why the heart-base is not a faculty, indriya. Objects do not impinge on the heart-base, the heart-base is not a doorway through which objects are experienced; it is not a "leader", a controlling principle in the experiencing of objects. The heart-base is different from the mind-door. The mind-door through which objects are experienced is a citta, the last bhavanga-citta arising before the mind-door adverting-consciousness which is the first citta of the mind-door process[2].

As regards mind faculty, manindriya, all eightynine types of citta are mind faculty. This faculty, unlike the five sense faculties, arises together with the realities it conditions by way of faculty-condition, indriya-paccaya. Citta is the "leader" in cognizing an object, in this field it rules over the associated dhammas. The accompanying cetasikas share the same object, but they do not cognize it in the same way as citta which is the leader. If there would be no citta, cetasikas could not arise; citta is the basis and foundation for the cetasikas. Citta conditions the accompanying cetasikas and also the rūpa it produces by way of conascent faculty-condition. When we gesticulate or speak there are rūpas conditioned by citta by way of faculty-condition; citta has controlling power over these rūpas. However, mind faculty does not last, it falls away immediately. We should not, while we speak or gesticulate, take the citta which produces rūpas for self. Neither should we take those rūpas for self; they arise because of conditions and fall away again. They do not belong to anyone.

The rebirth-consciousness, paṭisandhi-citta, conditions the accompanying cetasikas and the rūpa produced by kamma by way of conascent faculty-condition. Since it is the first citta in life it is too weak to produce rūpa, but kamma which produces this citta also produces rūpas at the same time.

The rūpas which are femininity faculty and masculinity faculty (itthindriya and purisindriya) have been classified as faculties, since they condition the characteristic marks, appearance and disposition of the sexes. However, they are not faculty-condition; they do not condition other phenomena by way of faculty-condition.

As to life faculty, jīvitindriya, there are two kinds: nāma-jīvitindriya and rūpa-jīvitindriya. Nāma-jīvitindriya which is a cetasika, one of the seven "universals"[3] arising with every citta, controls and maintains the life of the associated dhammas. It conditions the associated dhammas and the rūpa produced by them by way of faculty-condition.

As to rūpa-jīvitindriya, this is classified separately in the "Paṭṭhāna". This rūpa is always present in the groups of rūpa produced by kamma, such as the groups that include the senses. In the groups of rūpa produced by citta, temperature and

[2] See Appendix 1.

[3] The seven universals are the following cetasikas: contact (phassa), feeling (vedanā), remembrance or perception (saññā) volition (cetanā), concentration (ekaggatā cetasika), vitality (jīvita or jīvitindriya) and attention (manasikāra).

nutrition there is no jīvitindriya. Past kamma which produces rūpas, has fallen away, it is no longer present, and therefore, rūpa jīvitindriya, life-faculty, has a specific task: it maintains the life of the kamma-produced rūpas it has arisen together with in one group. It supports and maintains their life, it does not produce them. It maintains the other rūpas not at the moment of their arising, but during the moments of their presence, before they all fall away[4]. Life-faculty is related to the conascent rūpas by way of faculty-condition.

The five kinds of feelings which are pleasant bodily feeling (sukha), painful bodily feeling (dukkha), pleasant (mental) feeling (somanassa), unpleasant (mental) feeling (domanassa) and indifferent feeling (upekkhā) are faculties. Throughout our life feelings arise, feeling accompanies each citta. We can experience that bodily pain is a faculty, a "leader" or controlling principle in its own field. It controls the experiencing of the "flavour" of an unpleasant object and it can make us suffer intensely. Even though we are in pleasant surroundings we cannot rejoice when we suffer pain. At such a moment we cannot experience anything else but pain. Painful bodily feeling, pleasant bodily feeling, pleasant mental feeling, unpleasant (mental) feeling or indifferent feeling "govern" or rule over the citta and the other cetasikas they accompany; they condition them by way of conascent faculty-condition.

According to the "Visuddhimagga" (XIV, 128) pain makes the associated dhammas "wither" and pleasant bodily feeling "intensifies" the associated dhammas. Intensifying means strengthening, according to the Commentary. As to indifferent feeling, this does not make the accompanying dhammas wither nor does it intensify them. It is impartial in the experience of the object, according to the Commentary. Thus, it is more subtle in comparison with the other feelings.

We read in the "Visuddhimagga" (XVI, 10) about the functions of the faculties which are the five feelings:

> "... That of the faculties of pleasure, pain, joy and grief, is to govern conascent states and impart their own particular mode of grossness to those states. That of the equanimity faculty is to impart to them the mode of quiet, superiority and neutrality."

The two bodily feelings, pleasant bodily feeling and painful bodily feeling accompany body-consciousness which is vipākacitta. As we have seen, the vipākacittas which are the five pairs of sense-cognitions (seeing, hearing, etc.) do not produce rūpa. The three mental feelings, happy feeling, unhappy feeling and indifferent feeling, accompany cittas which produce bodily rūpas. They condition the citta and other cetasikas arising together with them and also mind-produced rūpa by way of faculty-condition. At rebirth, feeling that accompanies the vipākacitta which is rebirth-consciousness conditions that citta, the accompanying cetasikas and rūpa produced by kamma by way of faculty-condition. As we have seen, at that moment kamma produces rūpa.

We attach great importance to feeling, we let ourselves be carried away by the feelings which arise on account of pleasant or unpleasant objects we experience through the senses. If there would not be feelings on account of what we see, hear

---

[4] As we have seen, rūpa lasts as long as seventeen moments of citta: it has an arising moment, moments of presence and a moment of falling away.

or experience through the other senses, there would not be so much sorrow in life. We are enslaved to our feelings, but they are only realities which arise because of the appropriate conditions and do not last.

As we have seen, some of the faculties are rūpa and some are nāma. The faculties which are nāma condition other phenomena while they are conascent with them. The faculties which are the five senses have to arise prior to the nāmas they condition by way of faculty-condition. Without the sense-faculties the different objects which impinge on the senses cannot be experienced. Without the eye faculty visible object could not appear and without the ear faculty sound could not appear. The "world" appears through the six doorways because the faculties perform their functions. So long as we do not distinguish the sense faculties from each other we cling to a concept of self who can see and hear at the same time. In reality there is only one citta at a time which experiences one object. Each experience arises because of its appropriate conditions and falls away immediately, it is non-self. The following sutta stresses the importance of understanding the faculties which are the senses and the mind. They have to be understood as impermanent, dukkha and anattā. If they are not understood as they are, one cannot attain enlightenment. We read in the "Kindred Sayings" (V, Mahā-vagga, Book IV, Kindred Sayings on the Faculties, Ch III, paragraph 6, Stream-winner):

> "Monks, there are these six sense-faculties. What are the six? The sense-faculty of eye, that of ear, of nose, tongue, body and the sense-faculty of mind. These are the six sense-faculties. When the ariyan disciple understands, as they really are, the arising and the perishing of, the satisfaction in, the misery of and the escape from these six sense-faculties, such an ariyan disciple, monks, is called Streamwinner (sotāpanna), one not doomed to Purgatory[5], one assured, one bound for enlightenment.' "

Furthermore, there are five faculties sometimes referred to as "spiritual faculties". These are sobhana cetasikas (beautiful mental factors) included in the "factors of enlightenment" (bodhipakkiya dhammas) which should be developed for the attaining of enlightenment. They are: faith or confidence (saddhā), energy (viriya), mindfulness (sati), concentration (samādhi) and understanding (paññā). They control the accompanying dhammas and mind-produced rūpa, they condition them by way of faculty-condition. Among these five cetasikas energy and concentration can be akusala or sobhana, the other three are always sobhana, but as factors of enlightenment, all of them are sobhana. The five "spiritual faculties" condition the mahā-kusala cittas, mahā-vipākacittas and mahā-kiriyacittas they accompany and also mind produced rūpa by way of faculty-condition.

When the five spiritual faculties are developed in samatha they lead to the attainment of jhāna. When someone has accumulated skill in jhāna, different stages of rūpa-jhāna and arūpa-jhāna can be attained. The five spiritual faculties condition the rūpāvacara cittas and arūpāvacara cittas by way of faculty-condition. They also condition rūpa produced by these cittas, except in the case of arūpāvacara

[5] Hell, or hell planes. Existence in a hell plane is not eternal, therefore the translator uses "purgatory".

vipākacitta. Arūpāvacara vipākacitta does not produce rūpa since it arises in the arūpa-brahma planes where there is no rūpa.

The five spiritual faculties are also developed in vipassanā. They overcome their opposites. Faith or confidence in wholesomeness overcomes lack of confidence. Wholesomeness cannot be developed when we do not see its benefit. We may believe that we see the disadvantage of anger, but in the different situations in daily life we are negligent. Before we realize it we have spoken angry words and at such moments we do not see the disadvantage of akusala, we have no confidence in kusala. Kusala can be gradually developed; it can be accumulated, so that there will be more conditions for its arising. Energy which is wholesome overcomes indolence. The "Book of Analysis"(Ch 5, 123, 124) states about the faculty of energy:

> "Therein what is controlling faculty of energy? That which is the arousing of mental energy, toiling, endeavour, aspiring, effort, zeal, perseverance, vigour, stability, unfaltering endeavour, not relinquishing wish, not relinquishing the task, firm hold of the task, energy, controlling faculty of energy, power of energy. This is called controlling faculty of energy."

There is no self who exerts energy, energy is a cetasika, a faculty, arising because of its appropriate conditions. Energy is "not relinquishing the task". When one develops insight energy is not relinquishing the task of being mindful of nāma and rūpa, not shrinking back from considering their characteristics over and over again. The faculty of energy prevents one from losing courage even if one does not see much result. We cannot expect spectacular results immediately. The faculty of sati overcomes negligence of kusala, including negligence of developing right understanding of nāma and rūpa. Concentration overcomes distraction. In the development of insight it conditions the citta to attend to the reality appearing at the present moment. One should not force oneself to concentrate on any reality, because then one is bound to cling to a concept of self who concentrates. Concentration performs its function already while it arises together with right understanding. The faculty of paññā overcomes ignorance of the four noble Truths. The five spiritual faculties have to be developed together so that the four noble Truths can be realized.

These faculties will not develop merely by having faith in one's teacher, one has to develop them oneself. We read in the "Kindred Sayings" (V, Book IV, Kindred Sayings on the Faculties, Ch V, paragraph 4, Eastern Gatehouse) that the Buddha, while he was staying at Sāvatthī, in Eastern Garehouse, asked Sāriputta:

> "Do you believe, Sāriputta, that the controlling faculty of faith... of energy... of mindfulness... of concentration... that the controlling faculty of insight, if cultivated and made much of, plunges into the Deathless, has the Deathless for its goal, the Deathless for its ending?"

The "Deathless" is nibbāna. We read that Sāriputta answered:

> "In this matter, lord, I walk not by faith in the Exalted One, to wit: that the controlling faculty of faith... of energy... of mindfulness... of concentration... that the controlling faculty of insight, if cultivated and made much of, plunges into the Deathless, has the Deathless for its goal, the Deathless for its ending.

> They, lord, who have not realized, not seen, not understood, not made sure of, not attained this fact by insight, such may well walk by faith in others (in believing) that the controlling faculty of faith... that of insight, if cultivated and made much of, may so end.
>
> But, lord, they who have realized, seen, understood, made sure of, they who have attained this fact by insight, such are free from doubt, free from wavering, (in believing) that the controlling faculty of faith, of energy, of mindfulness, of concentration, of insight, if cultivated and made much of... will so end.
>
> But I, lord, have realized it, I have seen, understood and made sure of it, I have attained it by insight, I am free from doubt about it, that the controlling faculty of faith, of energy, of mindfulness, of concentration, of insight, does plunge into the Deathless, has the Deathless for its goal, the Deathless for its ending."

We then read that the Buddha approved of Sāriputta's words.

We read in the same section of the "Kindred Sayings" (paragraph 10, Faith) that the Buddha, while staying among the Angas at Market, asked Sāriputta:

> "Tell me, Sāriputta, could an ariyan disciple who is utterly devoted to, who has perfect faith in the Tathāgata, could an ariyan disciple have any doubt or wavering as to the Tathāgata or the Tathāgata's teaching?"

Sāriputta said that the ariyan disciple who has perfect faith in the Tathāgata could have no doubt as to the Tathāgata or his teaching and that he develops the controlling faculties of faith, energy, mindfulness, concentration and insight. We read that he said about the controlling faculty of insight:

> "Again, lord, of a faithful ariyan disciple who is established in mindfulness, whose thought is tranquillized, this may be expected: he will fully understand: A world without end is the round of rebirth. No beginning can be seen of beings hindered by ignorance, bound by craving, who run on, who fare on through the round of rebirth. The utter passionless ceasing of ignorance, of this body of darkness, is this blissful state, this excellent state, to wit:- the calming down of all the activities, the giving up of all bases (for rebirth), the destruction of craving, dispassion, cessation, nibbāna.' His insight, lord, is the controlling faculty of insight.
>
> Lord, that faithful ariyan disciple, thus striving and striving again, thus recollecting again and again, thus again and again composing his mind, thus clearly discerning again and again, gains utter confidence, when he considers: As to those things which formerly I had only heard tell of, now I dwell having experienced them in my own person: now by insight have I pierced them through and see them plain.' Herein, lord, his confidence is the controlling faculty of confidence."

We then read that the Buddha approved of Sāriputta's words.

We may find that the five "spiritual faculties" are still weak, and the reason is that also in the past they were weak, they have not been accumulated sufficiently. When we keep on listening to the Dhamma and considering what we heard, the five "spiritual faculties" can develop. They lead to the experiencing of the "Deathless", of nibbāna, but we do not know in which life that will happen. It is useless to have desire for the attainment of enlightenment, desire is counteractive to the development of understanding. We should only be intent on our task of this moment: developing more understanding of the reality which appears now.

There are three faculties which are lokuttara paññā. They control the purity of understanding at the moment of enlightenment and they condition the accompanying dhammas by way of conascent faculty-condition. The first one is the faculty of "I-shall-come-to-know-the-unknown"(an-aññātañ-ñassāmī't'indriya) and this is the lokuttara paññā which accompanies the magga-citta (lokuttara kusala citta) of the sotāpanna who attains the first stage of enlightenment. There are four stages of enlightenment: the stage of the sotāpanna (streamwinner), of the once-returner, the non-returner and the arahat. The sotāpanna comes to know what was not known before, nibbāna. Lokuttara paññā is conditioned by the sobhana cetasikas which have been accumulated from life to life. These cetasikas which are included in saṅkhārakkhandha (the khandha of "formations", consisting of all cetasikas except feeling and remembrance, saññā) are supporting one another and together they constitute the conditions for attaining enlightenment. It is encouraging to know that all good qualities such as generosity, patience and kindness, all the "perfections"[6] developed together with right understanding, are never lost. They have to be developed life after life and thus they can constitute the conditions for the realisation of the four noble Truths later on. When enlightenment is attained the lokuttara magga-citta eradicates defilements and experiences nibbāna

The second faculty which is lokuttara paññā is the "higher knowledge faculty"(aññindriya) which accompanies the phala-citta (fruition consciousness, lokuttara vipākacitta) of the sotāpanna, the magga-citta and the phala-citta of the sakadāgāmī (once-returner who has realised the second stage of enlightenment), and those of the anāgāmī (non-returner, who has realised the third stage of enlightenment), and also the magga-citta of the arahat.

The third faculty which is lokuttara paññā is the "faculty of him who knows" (aññātāvindriya) arising with the phala-citta of the arahat.

These three faculties which are lokuttara condition the lokuttara cittas and cetasikas they accompany by way of faculty-condition[7]. When the third lokuttara faculty arises there is nothing more to be realized, all defilements have been eradicated.

When the characteristics of conditioned dhammas are not yet fully known nibbāna cannot be realized. The "five spiritual faculties" have to be developed

---

[6] The Bodhisatta developed the "perfections" during aeons, with the purpose of becoming a Buddha. They are the following wholesome qualities: liberality, morality, renunciation, wisdom, energy, patience, truthfulness, determination, lovingkindness and equanimity.

[7] Realities can be considered under different aspects; they are a condition for other realities in different ways. When lokuttara paññā is considered under the aspect of faculty, as faculty-condition, there are three kinds. Lokuttara paññā is also a condition as Path factor.

during countless lives so that eventually the three faculties which are lokuttara can arise.

15 Jhāna-Condition

The word jhāna has been explained as being derived from "jhāyati", to contemplate, or to think closely of an object. Or else "jhāyati" can mean to burn (from another stem, jhāpana, Vis. IV, 119), since the jhāna-factors which are developed burn the "hindrances" (akusala cetasikas) away[1].

In the development of samatha specific cetasikas have to be developed so that jhāna, absorption, can be attained ("Visuddhimagga", Ch IV). They are the following five cetasikas:

- applied thinking (vitakka)
- sustained thinking (vicāra)
- rapture or interest (pīti)
- pleasant feeling (sukha)
- concentration (samādhi)

These cetasikas are sobhana (beautiful) cetasikas that are jhāna-factors assisting the citta to be absorbed in the meditation subject of jhāna. They have to be developed together with paññā which knows how to develop calm, so that absorption can be attained. When jhānacitta arises there are no longer sense impressions and there is temporary freedom from defilements. Jhānacitta is of a higher level of citta than kāmāvara citta, citta of the sense sphere.

The term jhāna in jhāna-condition is used in a wider sense than jhāna developed in samatha by means of the jhāna-factors that are the sobhana cetasikas mentioned above. The jhāna-factors that are jhāna-condition for the citta they accompany are not only the sobhana cetasikas developed in samatha; they arise with cittas which are kusala, akusala, vipāka or kiriya. The jhāna-factors in the sense of jhāna-condition assist the citta and the other cetasikas they accompany to be firmly fixed on the object that is experienced. Without the assistance of the jhāna-factors good or evil deeds cannot be performed.

The "Dhammasangaṇi" mentions in the "Summary" jhāna-factors arising not only with the mahā-kusala cittas which are accompanied by paññā, but also those arising with the mahā-kusala cittas which are unaccompanied by paññā, ñāṇa-vippayutta, as well as those arising with each of the akusala cittas[2].

We read in the "Paṭṭhāna" (Faultless Triplet, VII, Investigation Chapter, paragraph 431) that akusala jhāna-factors are related to their associated aggregates (the other nāmakkhandhas[3]) by jhāna-condition.

---

[1] The Atthasālinī (Expositor, Part V, Ch I, 167), with regard to contemplation of the object, uses the term upanijjhāna, and explains this as twofold: as closely examining the object, which are the meditation subjects of samatha; and as examining closely the characteristics of impermanence, dukkha and anattā. Insight, the Path and Fruition are called "characteristic examining jhāna".

[2] See paragraph 147 a and paragraph 397 a.

[3] The citta and cetasikas arising together with them.

There are seven jhāna-factors that are jhāna-condition and these include the five types of cetasikas mentioned above, but in this case they are not only sobhana cetasikas arising with sobhana citta. Summarizing them, they are:

- applied thinking (vitakka)
- sustained thinking (vicāra)
- rapture or interest (pīti)
- pleasant feeling (sukha)
- unpleasant feeling (domanassa)
- indifferent feeling (upekkhā)
- concentration (samādhi)

In this classification, pleasant feeling, unpleasant feeling and indifferent feeling are mentioned. Unpleasant feeling, domanassa, is always akusala. Apart from domanassa, the other jhāna-factors can arise with cittas which are kusala, akusala, vipāka or kiriya. The five pairs of sense-cognitions (seeing etc.) are not conditioned by jhāna-factors. The jhāna-factors assist citta each in their own way so that citta can be firmly fixed on an object.

Vitakka, applied thinking, "touches" the object which is experienced, it leads citta to the object (Vis. IV, 88). When vitakka is akusala it is wrong thinking. As to vicāra, sustained thinking, this has the characteristic of "continued pressure" on the object, it keeps citta "anchored" on it (Vis. IV, 88). Vitakka and vicāra accompany all cittas of the sense sphere, except the sense-cognitions and they condition the citta by way of jhāna-condition, so that it is firmly fixed on the object it experiences. Pīti, rapture, interest or enthusiasm, takes an interest in the object, it "refreshes" citta and cetasikas (Vis. IV, 94). In the case of cittas of the sense sphere, kāmāvacara cittas, it arises with all cittas which are accompanied by pleasant feeling. When it is akusala it accompanies lobha-mūla-citta; it conditions the lobha-mūlacitta by way of jhāna-condition. Sukha, in this context is the same as somanassa, pleasant feeling. Sukha, pleasant feeling, conditions the citta it accompanies by way of jhāna-condition. Domanassa, unpleasant feeling, can only accompany dosa-mūla-citta, citta rooted in aversion, and it assists the akusala citta to be fixed on the object in an unwholesome way. Upekkhā, indifferent feeling, which can be kusala, akusala, vipāka or kiriya, conditions the citta it accompanies by way of jhāna-condition. Samādhi, concentration, is the cetasika which is one-pointedness (ekaggatā). It has the function of focussing on one object and it accompanies every citta; it can be kusala, akusala, vipāka or kiriya. It causes the citta to be concentrated on the object it experiences. When samādhi is akusala it is wrong concentration, micchā-samādhi, and when it accompanies sobhana citta it is right concentration, sammā-samādhi.

The jhāna-factors condition the citta and cetasikas they accompany and the mind-produced rūpa by way of jhāna-condition and also at the moment of rebirth they condition the associated dhammas and kamma produced rūpa by way of jhāna-condition (Paṭṭhāna, Faultless Triplet, VII, Investigation Chapter, paragraph 431, VII a , b).

The subcommentary to the "Khandha-Vibhanga" (Book of Analysis I) explains the role of the jhāna-factors in relation to mind produced rūpa[4]. This subcommentary calls the jhāna-factors "strength-givers" (bala-dāyaka), they are intensifying factors which assist the citta and accompanying cetasikas to be fixed on an object. The jhāna-factors vitakka and vicāra play a specific role when citta produces speech-intimation. Do we know whether kusala vitakka or akusala vitakka conditions speech-intimation? When our objective is not dāna (generosity), sīla (morality) or bhāvanā (mental development), we speak with akusala citta and this happens time and again. When citta produces a facial expression of gladness, or when we smile, the jhāna-factor sukha plays its specific role, the jhāna-factor pīti (rapture) "refreshes" citta, in fact, all the accompanying jhāna-factors condition citta, the associated cetasikas and the rūpa produced by citta by way of jhāna-condition. When someone commits an unwholesome deed, such as killing, the dosa-mūlacitta, citta rooted in aversion, is conditioned by akusala jhāna-factors by way of jhāna-condition. It is accompanied by akusala vitakka which thinks of the object with violence, by vicāra which is occupied with the object in an unwholesome way, by unpleasant feeling and by concentration which causes the citta to be firmly fixed on the object. The akusala citta, the accompanying cetasikas and also the mind-produced rūpa are conditioned by akusala jhāna-factors,"strength-givers" or intensifying factors, by way of jhāna-condition. When we perform a generous deed, the kusala citta and accompanying cetasikas and also the mind produced rūpa are conditioned by sobhana jhāna-factors by way of jhāna-condition. These dhammas are also conditioned by root-condition, by faculty-condition and by several other conditions. Thus, as we have seen, jhāna-factors are not only operating while one cultivates samatha, they are conditions which function time and again in daily life, no matter whether we perform wholesome or unwholesome deeds.

The "Visuddhimagga" (Ch IV) mentions five jhāna-factors, in that case sobhana cetasikas, to be developed in samatha with the purpose of attaining jhāna. As we have seen, they are: applied thinking (vitakka), sustained thinking (vicāra),rapture or interest (pīti), pleasant feeling (sukha) and concentration (samādhi).

Paññā, right understanding, is indispensable in order to know the way to develop calm with a suitable meditation subject and to know the characteristics of those particular jhāna-factors. Paññā should know precisely when kusala citta arises and when akusala citta. There are forty meditation subjects of samatha and it depends on the individual which subject is suitable as a means to develop calm (Vis. Ch IV-Ch X).

The sobhana jhāna-factors have each their own function in inhibiting the hindrances so that calm can be developed. The hindrances are: sensuous desire (kāmacchanda), ill will (vyāpāda), sloth and torpor (thīna-middha), restlessness and regret (uddhacca-kukkucca) and doubt (vicikicchā).

Vitakka, applied thinking, "touches" the meditation subject; it thinks of it in the right way. Vicāra, sustained thinking, keeps the citta "anchored" on the meditation subject, reviewing it over and over again so that citta will remain fixed on the

---

[4] See "Abhidhamma Studies", IV, Mental Constituents, 3, Factors of Absorption, by Ven. Nyanaponika.

meditation subject. Vitakka inhibits the hindrances of sloth and torpor and vicāra inhibits the hindrance of doubt. Pīti, enthusiasm, takes an interest in the meditation subject so that one is not bored with it. It inhibits the hindrance which is ill will. Sukha which is developed in samatha is happy feeling concerning the meditation subject. It inhibits the hindrances which are restlessness and regret (uddhacca and kukkucca).

Samādhi, concentration, developed in samatha, is right concentration on the meditation subject. It inhibits the hindrance which is sensuous desire (kāmacchandha). As calm grows samādhi also develops. Concentration can be micchā-samādhi, wrong concentration, or sammā-samādhi, right concentration. Without paññā which knows precisely when kusala citta arises and when akusala citta, wrong concentration can be taken for right concentration. Someone may mistakenly believe that calm arises when he just sits and for example looks for a long time at a kasina (disk) which is among the meditation subjects of samatha. Instead of true calm which is wholesome, there is clinging to quietness.

Not merely intellectual understanding of the jhāna-factors is needed for the development of calm but also right understanding which discerns precisely their different characteristics when they arise. When one underestimates the difficulty of developing jhāna, wrong concentration is bound to arise. It is difficult to distinguish between different jhāna-factors such as vitakka and vicāra. While we are thinking, vitakka and vicāra perform their functions, they arise together; but do we discern their different characteristics? Do we know the characteristic of pīti, rapture, and can we distinguish it from sukha, pleasant feeling? When we find out for ourselves how difficult it is to distinguish between these jhāna-factors, we shall understand that a high degree of paññā is indispensable for the development of the jhāna-factors necessary for the attainment of the different stages of jhāna. When someone has attained the first stage of rūpa-jhāna[5], the rūpāvacara kusala citta is accompanied by all five jhāna-factors and these condition that citta by way of jhāna-condition. After having emerged from jhāna one has to review the jhāna-factors with mindfulness and right understanding (Vis. IV, 138). Also in samatha mindfulness and right understanding are needed but the aim is not, as is the case in vipassanā, to see realities as non-self. The aim of samatha is the temporary subduing of attachment to sense objects. The jhāna-factors are progressively abandoned as higher stages of jhāna are attained. A high degree of paññā is needed which discerns how to abandon the jhāna-factors which are more gross, so that higher stages of jhāna which are more refined and tranquil can be reached. In the beginning vitakka, applied thinking, and vicāra, sustained thinking, are still needed to become absorbed in the meditation subject, but as calm develops, these factors that are still gross can be abandoned. As higher stages are reached, pīti, rapture, and happy feeling, sukha, can be successively abandoned.

At the highest stage of rūpa-jhāna only the jhāna-factor samādhi is left and the accompanying feeling is indifferent feeling, upekkhā. At this stage calm is of a

[5] Fine-material jhāna. The meditation subjects of rūpa-jhāna are still dependent on materiality, whereas the meditation subjects of arūpa-jhāna, immaterial jhāna, are not.

higher degree and then upekkhā, which is more subtle than sukha, pleasant feeling, accompanies the jhānacitta.

The arūpāvacara cittas (of arūpa-jhāna, immaterial jhāna) are also accompanied by the jhāna-factor samādhi, and the accompanying feeling is indifferent feeling.

Jhāna-factors which are sobhana condition each kusala citta, and thus they also condition the kusala citta which develops vipassanā by way of jhāna-condition. In vipassanā the aim is not the suppression of the hindrances as is the case in samatha. Some people think that the hindrances have to be suppressed first before there can be right understanding of nāma and rūpa. In vipassanā, however, right understanding is developed of whatever reality appears, also when that reality is a "hindrance". When it appears it does so because it is conditioned. All conditioned realities have to be known as they are, as non-self. At the moment of right understanding of the characteristic of a hindrance such as desire or ill will, the citta is kusala citta and at that moment no hindrance arises.

There is no rule that samatha should be developed before vipassanā can be developed. Some people develop samatha, others do not, and this depends on conditions. People are born with different inclinations, different talents, different potentialities. Our life is an unbroken series of cittas and thus, inclinations can be accumulated from one moment to the next moment. The bhavanga-citta which succeeds the paṭisandhi-citta is conditioned by that citta by way of proximity-condition, anantara-paccaya, and each following citta is conditioned by the preceding one by way of proximity-condition. Cittas are conditioned by many different factors; there is no self who could alter the cittas which arise.

Lokuttara cittas are conditioned by sobhana jhāna-factors by way of jhāna-condition. The jhāna-factors are included in the enlightenment factors[6] which perform their functions so that enlightenment can be attained. The magga-citta (lokuttara kusala citta) eradicates defilements in accordance with the stage of enlightenment which is attained. The jhāna-factors condition the lokuttara citta to be steadfast and highly concentrated on the object which is nibbāna. Thus, nibbāna appears very clearly to the lokuttara citta and there is a high degree of calm.

Some people who attain enlightenment have developed samatha and attained jhāna, others have not. For those who have not developed jhāna before attaining enlightenment, the lokuttara cittas are accompanied by the jhāna-factors which are of the same degree as those of the first stage of jhāna. These cittas experience nibbāna with absorption concentration of the degree of the first stage of jhāna.

For those who are proficient in jhāna and also develop insight, jhānacitta can be the object of insight; jhāna is then the foundation of insight. In that way they can become detached from the idea that jhānacitta is self. We read in the "Kindred Sayings"(III, Khandhā-vagga, XXVIII, Kindred Sayings on Sāriputta, paragraph 1, Solitude) about a conversation between Sāriputta and Ānanda. We read that Ānanda said to Sāriputta:

---

[6] Bodhipakkhiya dhammas, wholesome qualities which should be developed for the attainment of enlightenment.

> " Calm are your senses, friend Sāriputta, clear and translucent the colour of your face. In what mood has the venerable Sāriputta been spending this day?'
>
> Friend, I have been dwelling aloof from passions, aloof from things evil, with my thought applied and sustained (with vitakka and vicāra) in first jhāna, which is born of solitude and full of zest (pīti) and happiness (sukha). To me thus, friend, the thought never came: It is I who am attaining first jhāna, or It is I who have attained first jhāna, or It is I who have emerged from first jhāna.'
>
> Surely for a long time have leanings to I-making, to mine-making and to vanity been well rooted out from the venerable Sāriputta. That is why it occurs not to the venerable Sāriputta: It is I who am attaining first jhāna, or It is I who have attained first jhāna, or It is I who have emerged from first jhāna.' "

In the following suttas we read that Sāriputta did not take the higher stages of rūpa-jhāna nor the stages of arūpa-jhāna for self.

For those who are proficient in jhāna and attain enlightenment, the lokuttara cittas can be accompanied by jhāna-factors of the different stages of jhāna, depending on the stage of jhāna which was the basis of insight just before enlightenment was attained. Since there are five stages of jhāna, the eight types of lokuttara cittas[7] can be accompanied by jhāna-factors of the five stages of jhāna[8], and thus there can be forty types of lokuttara cittas instead of eight types. For example, for someone who has attained enlightenment of the stage of the sotāpanna, streamwinner, the lokuttara magga-citta (lokuttera kusala citta) and the lokuttara phala-citta (fruition, lokuttara vipākacitta) can be accompanied by jhāna-factors of one of the five stages of jhāna, thus there can be ten types of lokuttara citta instead of two types. And it is the same for the following three stages of enlightenment. The degree and the amount of the jhāna-factors which condition a citta at a particular moment are variegated, and this is dependent on many different conditions.

The magga-citta (path-consciousness) is followed immediately, in the same process, by its result, the phala-citta (fruition-consciousness), and then, after that process is over, other types of citta which are not lokuttara but lokiya (worldly) arise. However, for those who are proficient in jhāna, who have jhāna as basis of insight, and have attained enlightenment with lokuttara jhānacittas, phala-cittas which experience nibbāna can arise again, many times during their life. This is not possible for those who attained enlightenment but who were not proficient in jhāna and did not have jhāna as basis of insight. However, for all those who have attained enlightenment defilements are progressively eradicated depending on the stage of enlightenment one has attained.

---

[7] At each of the four stages of enlightenment arise one type of lokuttara kusala citta and one type of lokuttara vipākacitta.

[8] See my "Abhidhamma in Daily Life", Ch. 23. As regards the four stages of arūpa-jhāna, they are accompanied by samādhi and upekkhā, indifferent feeling, just as in the case of the rūpa-jhānacittas of the fifth stage.

A high degree of paññā is needed for the development of the jhāna-factors so that jhāna can be attained. The disciples of the Buddha who were able to do so had accumulated a high proficiency in samatha during many lives. Instead of wishing for something that cannot be reached we should pay attention to what can be done right now. We can develop right understanding of the realities which have arisen already because of their own conditions. This kind of understanding leads to the eradication of defilements and that is the goal of the Buddha's teachings.

16 Path-Condition

In the case of path-condition, magga-paccaya, the cetasikas which are called path-factors are the conditioning dhammas (paccayas) and these are related to the dhammas arising together with them, the conditioned dhammas (paccayupanna dhammas), by way of path-condition, magga-paccaya. The path-factors which are path-condition are not merely the factors of the noble eightfold Path which leads to enlightenment, but the term path-factor should be taken in a wider sense. Path-factors can be akusala cetasikas which constitute the wrong path, or they can be sobhana cetasikas which constitute the right path.

The path-factors which are akusala cetasikas support the akusala citta and the other cetasikas they accompany to function as a path leading downwards, to an unhappy rebirth. The akusala path-factors support the akusala citta they accompany, for example, in killing or stealing.

The path-factors which are sobhana cetasikas support the kusala citta and the other cetasikas they accompany to function as a path leading to a happy rebirth. They support the kusala citta they accompany, for example, in the undertaking of dāna, the observing of sīla and in bhāvanā. Or they function as constituents of the noble eightfold Path leading to the end of the cycle of birth and death.

In the "Dialologues of the Buddha" (III, no. 33, The Recital, VIII) the path-factors of the wrong path are summed up as follows:

> "Eight wrong factors of character and conduct, to wit, wrong views, thinking, speech, action, livelihood, effort, mindfulness, concentration."

Not all eight factors of the wrong path are cetasikas which are path-condition. The four factors of wrong speech, wrong action, wrong livelihood and wrong mindfulness are not among the akusala cetasikas which are conditioning factors of path-condition. Wrong speech, wrong action and wrong livelihood are not specific cetasikas; they comprise different unwholesome actions motivated by akusala cetanā, unwholesome volition, which accompanies akusala citta. Wrong mindfulness does not function as path-condition; the cetasika mindfulness, sati, can only accompany sobhana citta, it cannot be akusala. Wrong mindfulness is a description of lack of mindfulness, lack of attention to kusala, of lobha.

The other four factors of the wrong path are the akusala cetasikas of wrong view, wrong thinking, wrong effort and wrong concentration. These cetasikas are conditioning factors of path-condition. We read in the "Paṭṭhāna" (Faultless Triplet, VII, Investigation Chapter, paragraph 432, IV) that akusala path-factors condition the akusala citta they accompany by way of path-condition. The text states:

> "Faulty state (akusala dhamma) is related to faulty state by path-condition. Faulty path-factors are related to their associated khandhas[1] by path-condition."

[1] The akusala cetasikas which are factors of the wrong path are included in the khandha of formations (saṅkhāra-kkhandha, which is all cetasikas except feeling and saññā, remembrance or perception). The associated khandhas are the akusala citta and the other cetasikas they accompany.

Wrong view (micchā-diṭṭhi) is an akusala cetasika arising with four types of lobha-mūla-citta[2]. Someone has wrong view about kamma and vipāka when he believes that good and bad deeds do not produce their appropriate results. It is wrong view to take realities for permanent or for "self". Wrong view conditions wrong practice of the Dhamma, it conditions taking the wrong path for the right path. This happens, for example, when someone believes that he should not be aware of akusala, that akusala should be suppressed before vipassanā can be developed. By understanding that akusala citta is conditioned by numerous factors, some of which are stemming from the past, and some of which are factors of the present, we can be reminded to be aware of akusala in order to see it as a conditioned nāma, not self.

When someone teaches wrong practice, wrong view conditions the rūpa that is speech intimation by way of path-condition. The "Paṭṭhāna" (in the same section, paragraph 432, V), under the heading of akusala dhamma which conditions indeterminate dhamma, states that akusala path-factors condition mind-produced rūpa by way of path-condition. As we have seen, indeterminate dhamma, avyākata dhamma, is neither kusala nor akusala; it comprises vipākacitta, kiriyacitta and rūpa. In the following definition indeterminate dhamma refers to rūpa. We read:

> "(V) Faulty state (akusala dhamma) is related to indeterminate state by path-condition.
>
> Faulty path-factors are related to mind-produced matter by path-condition."

Wrong thinking (micchā-saṅkappa) is the cetasika vitakka, thinking, which "touches" the object so that citta can cognize it. This factor conditions the akusala citta and cetasikas it accompanies by way of path-condition.

Wrong effort (micchā-vāyāma) is viriya cetasika which is akusala. It strengthens and supports the accompanying dhammas so that they can perform their functions in an unwholesome way, it conditions them by way of path-condition.

Wrong concentration (micchā-samādhi) is ekaggatā cetasika which conditions akusala citta to focus on the object in an unwholesome way, it conditions the accompanying dhammas by way of path-condition.

The factors of the wrong path perform each their own function as they condition citta, cetasikas and mind-produced rūpa by way of path-condition. The factors of the wrong path support by way of path-condition the citta and the other cetasikas they accompany to engage in wrong speech, wrong action and wrong livelihood. When we slander, the factors of the wrong Path condition speech intimation by way of path-condition. We can easily indulge in idle speech and this may not seem to be harmful. However, one kind of akusala can lead to other kinds of akusala by way of natural decisive support-condition, pakatūpanissaya paccaya, as we have seen[3]. Any degree of akusala is dangerous. The study of the factors of the wrong path can remind us to realize when we are on the wrong path which leads downwards.

---

[2] See Appendix 2.

[3] See Chapter 8.

Someone may take wrong effort for right effort and wrong concentration for right concentration. He may, for example, try very hard to focus on a particular object such as breath without right understanding of what breath is: a rūpa which is tangible object conditioned by citta. Or someone may think that he should try to concentrate on rūpas of the body and that he in that way can experience the arising and falling away of realities. The development of the eigthfold Path is the development of right understanding of any reality which appears because of conditions. If someone selects particular realities as objects of awareness or if he tries to apply himself to certain techniques in order to hasten the development of insight he is on the wrong path.

The factors of the right path are the following sobhana cetasikas:

- right view (sammā-diṭṭhi)
- right thinking (sammā-saṅkappa)
- right speech (sammā-vācā)
- right action (sammā-kammanta)
- right livelihood (sammā-ājīva)
- right effort (sammā-vāyāma)
- right mindfulness (sammā-sati)
- right concentration (sammā-samādhi)

We read in the "Paṭṭhāna" (Faultless Triplet, VII, Investigation Chapter, paragraph 432) that the path-factors which are kusala condition the citta and the other cetasikas they accompany by way of path-condition. They also condition the mind-produced rūpa, which is indeterminate dhamma (neither kusala nor akusala), by way of path-condition. The Paṭṭhāna states this under the following three headings: kusala dhamma conditions (other) kusala dhammas, kusala dhamma conditions indeterminate dhamma (namely rūpa, produced by citta), kusala dhamma conditions (other) kusala dhammas and indeterminate dhamma (rūpa, produced by citta):

> "(I) Faultless state (kusala dhamma) is related to faultless state by path-condition.
>
> Faultless path factors are related to (their) associated khandhas by path-condition.
>
> (II) Faultless state is related to indeterminate state by path-condition.
>
> Faultless path-factors are related to mind-produced matter by path-condition.
>
> (III) Faultless state is related to faultless and indeterminate state by path-condition.
>
> Faultless path-factors are related to (their) associated khandhas and mind-produced matter by path-condition."

The factors of the right path are sobhana cetasikas which condition sobhana citta by way of path-condition. Thus, they condition sahetuka cittas (cittas with roots). We read in the same section of the "Paṭṭhāna" (paragraph 432) that they condition mahā-vipākacittas (resultant indeterminate) and mahā-kiriyacittas (functional indeterminate) by way of path-condition:

> "Resultant indeterminate or functional indeterminate path factors are related to (their) associated aggregates and mind-produced matter by path condition."

The sobhana pathfactors condition rūpāvacara cittas and arūpāvacara cittas that are kusala vipāka and kiriya by way of path-condition. They also condition lokuttara cittas by way of path-condition[4].

Not all path-factors arise with each kind of sobhana citta. Some types of sobhana citta are accompanied by paññā and some are not. One may, for example, perform deeds of generosity with right understanding or without right understanding. When kusala citta without right understanding arises, it is not conditioned by the path-factor sammā-diṭṭhi. The performing of wholesome deeds without the development of right understanding of nāma and rūpa can lead to a happy rebirth, but it does not lead to the eradication of the wrong view of self and of the other defilements, and thus, it does not lead to freedom from rebirth.

The path-factor sammā-diṭṭhi can have many degrees. It can be intellectual understanding of kusala and akusala and their results, it can be paññā which directly understands kusala as kusala and akusala as akusala, or it can be right understanding of nāma and rūpa as non-self. Only right understanding of the true nature of nāma and rūpa will lead to detachment from the wrong view of "self" and from all realities, to freedom from the cycle of birth and death. When the noble eightfold Path which leads to the end of rebirth is being developed the object of paññā is a nāma or rūpa which appears at the present moment. Through mindfulness of realities appearing in our daily life sammā-diṭṭhi of the eightfold Path can come to see them as they are, as non-self.

Sammā-saṅkappa, right thinking, is vitakka cetasika which is sobhana. It assists each kusala citta which is intent on wholesomeness, it "touches" the object of wholesomeness. It conditions sobhana citta by way of path-condition. When right thinking is a factor of the noble eightfold Path it has to accompany right understanding, paññā. Right thinking "touches" the nāma or rūpa which appears so that paññā can understand it as it is. As we have seen (in chapter 14), this cetasika also functions as jhāna-condition for the accompanying dhammas. A reality can condition other realities in more than one way.

There are three cetasikas which are sīla, namely: right speech, right action and right livelihood. They are actually the three abstinences or virati cetasikas which are:

- abstinence from wrong speech (vacīduccarita virati)
- abstinence from wrong action (kāyaduccarita virati)
- abstinence from wrong livelihood (ājīvaduccarita virati)

They may, one at a time, accompany kusala citta when the occasion arises. They do not accompany each kusala citta. While we abstain from wrong action or speech there can be awareness and right understanding of nāma and rūpa. Paññā can realize that the cetasika which abstains from akusala is non-self, that it arises because of its appropriate conditions.

---

[4] See Appendix 2 for details about these cittas.

The three abstinences which accompany cittas of the sense-sphere, kāmāvacara cittas, arise only one at a time. When abstinence of wrong speech arises, there cannot be at the same time abstinence from wrong action. However, when lokuttara citta arises all three abstinences accompany the lokuttara citta and then nibbāna is the object. The abstinences which are lokuttara are the right speech, the right action and the right livelihood of the supramundane eightfold Path. They fulfill their function of path-factors by eradicating the conditions for wrong speech, wrong action and wrong livelihood. Thus, the object of the abstinences which are lokuttara is different from the object of the abstinences which accompany cittas of the sense-sphere. The path-consciousness, magga-citta, eradicates the tendencies to evil conduct subsequently at the stages of enlightenment. The magga-citta (path-consciousness) as well as the phala-citta (fruition-consciousness), which is the result of the magga-citta and immediately succeeds it in the same process, are accompanied by all three abstinences. Right action, right speech and right livelihood do not accompany the mahā-kiriyacitta of the arahat. He has eradicated all akusala and therefore there is no need for him to abstain from akusala. Neither do the three abstinences accompany jhānacitta since the jhānacitta is remote from sense impressions and there is thus no opportunity to abstain from the defilements connected with sense impressions.

Sammā-vāyāma or right effort is another factor of the right path. It is viriya cetasika (energy or effort) which strengthens and supports the accompanying dhammas so that they are intent on kusala. When it accompanies right understanding of the noble eightfold Path it is energy and courage to persevere being aware of nāma and rūpa which appear one at a time through the six doorways. At the moment of mindfulness of nāma and rūpa, right effort has arisen already because of conditions and it performs its function; we do not need to think of making an effort. When we think, "I can exert effort, I can strive", with an idea of self who can do so, akusala citta has arisen with clinging to reach the goal. Wrong effort may arise without our noticing it. Right effort, when it accompanies right understanding, supports the other factors of the eightfold Path, but we should remember that it arises because of its own conditions, that it is non-self.

We read in the "Gradual Sayings" (Book of the Threes, Ch V, paragraph 49, Ardent energy):

> "Monks, on three occasions ardent energy is to be exerted. What three?
>
> To prevent the arising of evil, unprofitable states not yet arisen; to cause the arising of good, profitable states not yet arisen; to endure bodily feelings that have arisen, feelings which are painful, sharp, bitter, acute, distressing and unwelcome, which drain the life away. These are the three occasions...
>
> Now when a monk exerts himself on these three occasions, he is called strenuous, shrewd and mindful for making an end of dukkha.' "

This sutta reminds us that right effort has to accompany right understanding, so that all the conditioning factors leading to the end of dukkha can be developed. Sickness and pain are bound to arise because we are born; we cannot control our body. Also at such moments right understanding can be developed. Then right effort performs its function of supporting the associated dhammas.

Sammā-sati, right mindfulness, is non-forgetfulness of what is wholesome. Mindfulness arises with each sobhana citta. There is mindfulness of the levels of dāna, sīla and bhāvanā. When sati arises it is a condition for seeing the value of kusala and the disadvantage of akusala. We may have aversion towards someone else's words and behaviour and we are about to answer back. But when mindfulness arises and we see that aversion is ugly, we may refrain from speaking unpleasant words. At such a moment we are considerate of the other person's feelings and we do not think of ourselves.

Sati of the level of satipaṭṭhāna is right mindfulness of the nāma or rūpa which appears so that understanding of that reality as non-self can be developed. Mindfulness does not last, it arises just for a moment, but it can be accumulated. Mindfulness and right understanding cannot arise without the appropriate conditions: listening to the teachings as explained by the right friend in Dhamma, considering what one has heard and applying it in daily life. Moreover, all wholesome qualities developed together with satipaṭṭhāna are supportive conditions for paññā. When we learn to be less selfish and develop kindness, thoughtfulness and patience, these qualities support paññā to become detached from the idea of self. Sati that accompanies right understanding of the eightfold Path is a factor of the noble eightfold Path.

Sammā-samādhi, right concentration, is another path-factor accompanying sobhana citta. Kusala citta which is intent on dāna, sīla or bhāvanā is accompanied by right concentration which conditions the citta and accompanying cetasikas to focus on an object in the wholesome way. Right concentration which is a factor of the noble eightfold Path has to accompany right understanding of the eightfold Path.

We read in the "Kindred Sayings" (V, Mahā-vagga, XLV, Kindred Sayings on the Way, Ch III, Perversion, paragraph 8, Concentration) that the Buddha, while he was at Sāvatthī, said to the monks[5] :

> "Bhikkhus, I will teach you noble right concentration with its supports and accessories. Listen to that...
>
> And what, bhikkhus, is noble concentration with its supports and accessories? There are...right view... right mindfulness. The one-pointedness of mind equipped with these seven factors is called noble right concentration with its supports,' and also with its accessories' "

When paññā realizes the true nature of the nāma or rūpa which appears, right concentration assists the citta and the accompanying cetasikas to cognize that object. As we have seen, right concentration also conditions the sobhana citta and cetasikas it accompanies by way of jhāna-condition.

When right understanding of nāma and rūpa is being developed, the other path-factors develop as well together with right understanding. Some people believe that one should first develop sīla and samatha before one develops vipassanā, right understanding of nāma and rūpa. All kinds of wholesomeness are beneficial and they

[5] I used the translation by Venerable Bodhi.

can be developed along with right under- standing. However, there is no particular order according to which different ways of kusala should be developed. It depends on the accumulations of the individual, on natural decisive support-condition, and on other conditions which type of kusala citta arises at a particular moment. When right understanding of the eightfold Path arises the object experienced at that moment is a nāma or rūpa which appears.

Paññā of the eightfold Path develops very gradually in the course of countless lives. When we consider realities which appear in daily life and begin to be mindful of them, right understanding of nāma and rūpa develops. By the development of the eightfold Path enlightenment can eventually be attained and defilements can be eradicated stage by stage. The path-factors of the noble eightfold Path lead to deliverance from the cycle of birth and death. When the last stage of enlightenment, the stage of the arahat, has been realized, all defilements are eradicated and there will not be rebirth for him.

17 Three Pairs of Conditions

There are six conditions which form three pairs and of each pair the two conditions have characteristics opposite to each other. These conditions are in part similar to previously mentioned conditions, but they each manifest a different aspect of conditional relations between realities. The three pairs are the following:

- association-condition, sampayutta-paccaya
- dissociation-condition, vippayutta-paccaya

- presence-condition, atthi-paccaya
- absence-condition, natthi-paccaya

- disappearance-condition, vigata-paccaya
- non-disappearance-condition, avigata-paccaya

With regard to association-condition, we read in the "Paṭṭhāna" (II, Analytical Exposition of Conditions, 19):

> "The four immaterial aggregates (nāmakkhandhas) are mutually related to one another by association-condition."

Association-condition, sampayutta-paccaya, only pertains to nāma, to citta and its accompanying cetasikas. We read in the "Visuddhimagga" (XVII, 94) about this condition:

> "Immaterial states (nāma dhammas) that assist by the kind of association consisting in having the same physical basis (vatthu), the same object, the same arising, the same cessation, are association-conditions, according as it is said, The four immaterial khandhas are a condition, as association-condition, for each other' (Paṭṭhāna, I, 6)."

Seeing, for example, arises together with the associated cetasikas at the same vatthu, the eye-base; seeing and the associated cetasikas experience visible object through the eye-door and then they fall away together. Citta and cetasikas condition one another by way of association-condition, but they each perform their own funcion. Seeing-consciousness cognizes visible object, it is the "chief" in knowing the object. Feeling experiences the "flavour" of the object, saññā marks or recognizes the object, and the other "universals"[1] perform their own functions. The eyesense which is the base, the physical place of origin (vatthu) for seeing, is also doorway (dvāra), that is, the means through which citta and cetasikas experience the object. Only in the case of the five pairs of sense-cognitions (seeing, hearing, etc.) the same rūpas, namely the five senses, are both doorway and base. All the other cittas, apart from the sense-cognitions, arise at the heart-base (hadaya-vatthu). Each citta and its accompanying cetasikas arise together at the same base, experience the same object and fall away together.

The citta and cetasikas which condition one another by way of association-condition, sampayutta-paccaya, also condition one another by way of conascence,

---

[1] The seven cetasikas which arise with each citta, namely, contact, feeling, perception (saññā), volition, concentration, life-faculty and attention.

sahajāta. However, association-condition is not identical with conascence-condition. Conascence-condition also pertains to rūpas which arise together and to nāma and rūpa which arise together[2]. Association-condition, in contrast, only pertains to nāmas, citta and cetasikas, which arise together and condition one another.

Association-condition manifests the close association between citta and cetasikas. Although in the planes where there are five khandhas (nāma and rūpa) citta and cetasikas arise together with rūpa, they are not associated with rūpa in the same way as they are with each other. Feeling, for example, is nāma, it is closely associated with citta and the other cetasikas. When lobha-mūla-citta accompanied by pleasant feeling enjoys a pleasant sound, the accompanying cetasikas share the same object, and they are all affected by the pleasant feeling, they are conditioned by it by way of association-condition. Citta and the accompanying cetasikas are of a great diversity since each of them conditions the other nāma-dhammas by way of association-condition. Kusala citta which is accompanied by sobhana cetasikas is quite different from akusala citta which is accompanied by akusala cetasikas. Some cetasikas can accompany cittas which are kusala, akusala, vipāka or kiriya, but they are of a different quality in each of these cases. Effort or energy (viriya), for example, which is kusala, such as energy for generosity or for awareness at this moment, is quite different from energy which is akusala, such as wrong effort accompanying attachment. Wrong effort arises, for example, when one tries very hard to concentrate on particular objects of awareness in order to attain a quick result of one's practice.

As regards dissociation-condition, vippayutta-paccaya, we read in the "Paṭṭhāna" (II, Analytical Exposition of Conditions, 20):

> "The material states (rūpas) are related to the immaterial states (nāmas) by dissociation-condition.
>
> The immaterial states are related to the material states by dissociation-condition."

This condition is altogether different from association-condition, because it pertains to rūpa which conditions nāma and to nāma which conditions rūpa. The nature of nāma is completely different from the nature of rūpa, they cannot condition one another by way of association. They cannot be as closely associated as citta and cetasika which are both nāma arising together at the same physical base, experiencing the same object, and falling away together.

In the case of dissociation-condition, the conditioning factor can arise at the same time as the reality it conditions, it can arise before it or it can arise after it. Thus, dissociation-condition can be conascent, prenascent or postnascent. As regards conascent dissociation-condition, when citta produces rūpa such as speech intimation, that rūpa arises together with the citta, it is conditioned by citta by way of conascence-condition and also by way of conascent dissociation-condition. Although citta and the rūpa it produces arise together, they are each of a different nature and therefore, they are dissociated.

[2] See chapter 5.

In the case of prenascent dissociation-condition, the conditioning factors, which are the sense-bases and the heart-base, have to arise before the conditioned dhamma, the citta which is dependent on them; thus, they condition citta by way of prenascent dissociation-condition. As we have seen, the heart-base at the first moment of life arises at the same time as the paṭisandhi-citta[3], it is conditioned by citta by way of conascent dissociation-condition. During life, however, the heart-base arises before the citta which is dependent on it[4].

When we feel pain we can be reminded that the body-base (bodysense) is rūpa which is dissociated from painful feeling which is nāma; the body-base conditions the painful feeling by way of prenascent dissociation-condition. When nāma and rūpa are not distinguished from each other we cling to a "whole" of mind and body, we take them for "mine" or "self" and they seem to last. We keep on thinking of "my sensitive body" and "my painful feeling". The body-base which is the base for body-consciousness and the accompanying painful feeling, is only an infinitesimal rūpa which arises and falls away. Painful feeling does not last either, it falls away immediately. Thus, when we think of our painful feeling it has gone already. Through satipaṭṭhāna one can learn to distinguish the characteristic of nāma from the characteristic of rūpa, and then we shall be less inclined to think of a self who feels pain.

We read in the "Kindred Sayings" (V, Book VIII, Kindred Sayings about Anuruddha, Ch II, paragraph 10, Grievously afflicted):

> "On a certain occasion the venerable Anuruddha was staying near Sāvatthī in Dark Wood, being sick and grievously afflicted.
>
> Now a number of monks came to visit the venerable Anuruddha, and on coming to him... said this:
>
> Pray what is the venerable Anuruddha's life, in that the painful feelings that come upon him make no impression on his mind?'
>
> Friends, it is because I dwell with my mind well grounded in four arisings of mindfulness. That is why the painful feelings that come upon me make no impression on my mind. What are the four?
>
> Herein, friends, I dwell in body contemplating body, being ardent, self-possessed and mindful. So with regard to feelings... mind... dhammas...
>
> It is because I thus dwell, friends, that the painful feelings that come upon me make no impression on my mind.' "

In the case of dissociation-condition which is postnascent, the conditioning dhamma arises after the dhamma it conditions. We have seen under the section on postnascence-condition, pacchajāta-paccaya (Ch 9), that citta consolidates the

---

[3] Both the heart-base and the paṭisandhi-citta are produced by kamma at the same time. See Ch. 5.

[4] The rūpas which are the five sense objects have to arise prior to the citta which is dependent on them. They are external objects cognized by citta and the relation between the object and citta is not that of dissociation-condition. Therefore, they are not included in prenascent dissociation-condition. See U Nārada, Guide to Conditional Relations, Ch II, 20 c, Base-Prenascence-Dissociation.

rūpas of the body which have arisen previously to it and have not fallen away yet. Citta also conditions these rūpas by way of postnascent dissociation-condition. The citta which conditions the rūpas of the body in this way is altogether different from these rūpas, it is "dissociated" from rūpa.

The second pair is presence-condition, atthi-paccaya, and absence-condition, natthi-paccaya. With regard to presence-condition, atthi-paccaya, the conditioning dhamma consolidates the conditioned dhamma by its presence. The dhamma which conditions another dhamma in this way can arise at the same time as the conditioned dhamma, it can arise prior to it or after it.

In the case of conascent presence-condition, the same conditioning dhammas and conditioned dhammas which are related by conascence-condition, sahajāta-paccaya, are also related by conascent presence-condition. As we have seen (in Ch 5), the dhammas that cause the simultaneous arising of other dhammas condition those by way of conascence.

The following dhammas are mutually related by conascence-condition and by conascent presence-condition: citta and cetasikas that arise together; the four great Elements; the rebirth-consciousness and the heart-base[5].

Furthermore, there are dhammas that condition other dhammas by way of conascence-condition and by conascent presence-condition, without their being mutually related in these ways. This is the case for the following dhammas that are conascence-condition and conascent presence-condition for the dhammas they condition: the rebirth-consciousness for the rūpas other than the heartbase produced by kamma at that moment[6]; citta for the rūpa it produces; the four great Elements of Earth (solidity), Water (cohesion), Fire (heat) and Wind (motion) for the "derived rūpas", the rūpas other than the four great Elements[7].

Conascent presence-condition seems to be identical with conascence-condition. However, the teaching of conascent presence-condition reminds us of the fact that the dhamma which conditions another conascent dhamma is still present, that it has not fallen away yet.

As regards prenascent presence-condition, this pertains to the rūpas which are bases, vatthus, and the rūpas which are the sense objects and which condition the citta by way of object-condition. The rūpas which are bases and objects condition

---

[5] When the conditioning dhammas and the conditioned dhammas are mutually dependent, they are not only related by way of conascence, but also by way of mutuality, aññamañña (see Ch 5).

[6] In the case of human birth, kamma produces at the moment of rebirth three decads, groups of rūpa: one with the heartbase, one with bodysense and one with sex. The rebirth-consciousness arising at the same time as these rūpas conditions them by way of conascence-condition. The rebirth-consciousness and the heartbase are mutually dependent, but this is not so in the case of the rebirth-consciousness and the other rūpas produced by kamma at that moment.

[7] In these cases there is no mutual relationship: the citta that produces rūpa is not dependent on that rūpa for its arising. Evenso, the four Great Elements are not dependent on the conascent derived rūpas for their arising.

citta after having arisen prior to it, thus they are prenascent to the citta they condition[8].

The term prenascence-condition may not tell us whether a conditioning reality is still present to the reality it conditions. The teaching of prenascent presence-condition shows us that, although the conditioning reality has arisen previously, it is still present when it conditions another reality. Visible object conditions seeing by way of prenascent presence-condition. It has arisen before seeing, but when it is experienced by seeing it is still present. The other cittas of the eye-door process also experience visible object which is still present. Seeing arises at the eye-base and it is conditioned by this rūpa by way of prenascent presence-condition. Learning about the base and the object which condition seeing helps us to understand the truth of anattā, non-self. There is no self who can cause eye-base and visible object to arise at the right moment, prior to seeing, and to condition seeing while they are still present.

Presence-condition can also be postnascent. Citta consolidates rūpas of the body which have previously arisen but have not fallen away yet by way of postnascence-condition[9] and by way of postnascent presence-condition. The teaching of postnascent presence-condition shows us that citta and the rūpas of the body it consolidates are still present to each other.

The "Paṭṭhāna" (Faultless Triplet, Investigation Chapter, paragraph 435, VII, d,e) mentions food and also physical life-faculty (rūpa-jīvitindriya) separately under presence-condition. We read:

> "Edible food is related to this body by presence-condition.
>
> Physical life-faculty is related to kamma-produced rūpa by presence-condition."

After edible food has been taken and it has pervaded the body, the nutritive essence it contains supports the internal nutritive essence present in the groups of rūpa of the body, so that new groups of rūpa can be produced[10]. When we consider the relation of nutrition to the body, it helps us to see that life can go on because of conditions. The rūpa which is nutritive essence present in each group of rūpas of the body can produce new rūpas, but it cannot do so without the support of the nutritive essence present in food. Nutritive essence is one of the four factors which can produce rūpas of the body, the other being kamma, citta and temperature. Edible food conditions the rūpas of the body by way of presence-condition, it supports and consolidates them.

As regards physical life faculty, rūpa-jīvitindriya, this is always present in the groups of rūpa produced by kamma. It does not occur in the groups of rūpa produced by citta, heat or nutrition. Past kamma which is one of the factors that produces rūpas of the body is not present to those rūpas in the same way as the

---

[8] Rūpa cannot at its arising moment condition citta since it is then too weak. It can only condition citta after it has arisen, thus, at the moments of its presence. Therefore, it has to arise prior to the citta it conditions. Rūpa lasts as long as seventeen moments of citta. See Appendix 1 for the process of cittas which experience a sense object.

[9] See Ch 9.

[10] Nutritive essence is one of the eight inseparable rūpas present in each group of rūpas.

other three factors which produce rūpas of the body: citta, temperature and nutrition. A deed, done in the past has fallen away, but the intention or volition which motivated that deed is accumulated from moment to moment. The force of past kamma is carried on and therefore kamma still has the power to produce rūpa at present. Since past kamma which produces rūpas, has fallen away and is no longer present, rūpa jīvitindriya, life-faculty, has a specific task: it maintains the life of the kamma-produced rūpas it has arisen together with in one group. It supports and maintains their life, it does not produce them. It maintains the other rūpas not at the moment of their arising, but during the moments of their presence, before they all fall away. Eyesense, for example, is produced by kamma, and thus there must also be jīvitindriya together with it in that group of rūpas produced by kamma. The same is true for the other senses.

We read about life faculty in the "Visuddhimagga" (XIV, 59):

> "The life faculty has the characteristic of maintaining conascent kinds of matter[11]. Its function is to make them occur. It is manifested in the establishing of their presence. And although it has the capacity consisting in the characteristic of maintaining, etc., yet it only maintains conascent kinds of matter at the moment of presence, as water does lotuses and so on. Though dhammas arise due to their own conditions, it maintains them, as a wet-nurse does a prince..."

Life faculty takes as a "wetnurse" the place of kamma, the "mother", in maintaining the life of the kamma-produced rūpas. Life faculty maintains the life of the rūpas it arises together with in a group, it consolidates them; it maintains the other rūpas, not at the moment of their arising, but during the moments of their presence, before they fall away together. Life faculty performs its task of consolidating kamma-produced rūpas from birth to death, it conditions them by way of presence-condition.

Life faculty is a condition for distinguishing kamma-produced rūpa from other kinds of rūpa. We cling to the body which is alive, we cling to eyesense and earsense and take them for self. They are only elements produced by kamma and maintained by life faculty, a kind of rūpa which is not self. They arise only because there are the appropriate conditions for their arising. When we lose eyesense or earsense it is evident that there are no longer conditions for the arising of these kamma-produced rūpas.

As regards absence-condition, natthi-paccaya, this condition is similar to proximity-condition, anantara-paccaya, and contiguity-condition, samanantara-condition[12]. The citta which falls away conditions the arising of the next one by way of proximity-condition and contiguity-condition. However, the next citta can only arise when the preceding one has fallen away, when it is absent. Absence does not mean that the citta was never there; it means that the citta that has just fallen away assists by its absence the citta arising next to it; after it has fallen away it gives the next citta the opportunity to arise without any interval.

---

[11] Life faculty arises together with other rūpas in a group and it maintains these rūpas.

[12] See Ch. 4.

The "Paṭṭhāna" (Analytical Exposition, II, 23) refers to the arising and falling away of cittas in contiguity; the citta with its accompanying cetasikas that has just fallen away conditions the following citta with its accompanying cetasikas by way of absence-condition:

> "States, citta and cetasikas, which have just disappeared in contiguity, are related to present states, citta and cetasikas, by absence-condition."

Only one citta at a time arises and then falls away, but cittas succeed one another from birth to death, and death is followed by rebirth. The cycle of birth and death continues until all defilements have been eradicated and one finally passes away.

The third pair of conditions is disappearance-condition, vigata-paccaya, and non-disappearance-condition, avigata-paccaya. Disappearance-condition is similar to absence-condition. Non-disappearance-condition is similar to presence-condition. Similar conditions have been given different names, "as an embellishment of teaching to suit the needs of those who are teachable", the "Visuddhimagga" (XVII, 100) states.

Disappearance-condition is similar to absence-condition but the word disappearance helps us to understand that the absence of the conditioning dhamma does not mean that it never was. Disappearance-condition also refers to the condition whereby the citta that has fallen away conditions the arising of the next citta. The word disappearance helps us to understand that the preceding citta, which is the conditioning dhamma, after it has reached its cessation moment, gives the opportunity for the arising of the subsequent citta, the conditioned dhamma, without any interval. As we have seen (Ch 5), each moment of citta can be divided into three extremely short periods: the moment of its arising, the moment of its presence and the moment of its cessation. The preceding citta must have reached its cessation moment so as to condition the subsequent citta since only one citta arises at a time.

Non-disappearance-condition is similar to presence-condition. In the case of presence-condition the conditioning dhamma assists the conditioned dhamma by its presence, and in the case of non-disappearance-condition the conditioning dhamma assists the conditioned dhamma by virtue of not having reached cessation. A dhamma which has not yet disappeared can, while it is still present, condition other dhammas. However, the conditioning dhamma cannot stay on, it has to fall away. Just as in the case of presence-condition, the conditioning dhamma can be prenascent, conascent or postnascent to the dhamma it conditions by way of non-disappearance-condition.

18 Aspects of the Twenty-Four Conditions

Summarizing the twenty-four conditions, they are:

- root-condition (hetu-paccaya)
- object-condition (ārammaṇa-paccaya)
- predominance-condition (adhipati-paccaya)
- proximity-condition (anantara-paccaya)
- contiguity-condition (samanantara-paccaya)
- conascence-condition (sahajāta-paccaya)
- mutuality-condition (aññamañña-paccaya)
- dependence-condition (nissaya-paccaya)
- decisive support-condition (upanissaya-paccaya)
- prenascence-condition (purejāta-paccaya)
- postnascence-condition (pacchājāta-paccaya)
- repetition-condition (āsevana-paccaya)
- kamma-condition (kamma-paccaya)
- vipāka-condition (vipāka-paccaya)
- nutriment-condition (āhāra-paccaya)
- faculty-condition (indriya-paccaya)
- jhāna-condition (jhāna-paccaya)
- path-condition (magga-paccaya)
- association-condition (sampayutta-paccaya)
- dissociation-condition (vippayutta-paccaya)
- presence-condition (atthi-paccaya)
- absence-condition (natthi-paccaya)
- disappearance-condition (vigata-paccaya)
- non-disappearance-condition (avigata-paccaya)

The Buddha taught how every reality which arises is dependent on conditions. These conditions are not abstractions, they operate now, in our daily life. What we take for our mind and our body are mere elements which arise because of their appropriate conditions and are devoid of self. We should consider the conditions for the bodily phenomena which arise and fall away all the time. At the first moment of our life kamma produced the heart-base and other rūpas together with the rebirth-consciousness, and throughout our life kamma continues to produce the heartbase and the sense-bases. Not only kamma, but also citta, heat and nutrition produce rūpas of the body. When we touch the body hardness appears, but this is only an element which arises and falls away; nobody can cause its arising and it does not belong to "our body". Through awareness of realities we shall understand more clearly the truth that what we call "our body" are fleeting elements which arise because of their own conditions.

The cittas which arise are dependent on many different conditions. Cittas succeed one another without any interval. Seeing arises time and again and after seeing has fallen away akusala cittas usually arise. We cling to visible object, or we take it for a being or a person. Defilements arise because they have been accumulated and they are carried on, from moment to moment, from life to life. They are a natural decisive support-condition, pakatūpanissaya-paccaya, for akusala citta arising at this moment. Akusala has become our nature, but if we see the disadvantage of akusala, there are conditions for the development of right understanding which can eradicate akusala.

We are so used to the idea of seeing living beings, people and animals, and we do not realize that we are deluded about reality because of our accumulated ignorance and wrong view. When we watch T.V. and we see people moving, we know that there are no people there. There are rapidly changing projected images on a screen and this gives us the illusion that there are people who are acting. These images are merely different colours which appear through the eyesense; on account of what we see we think of concepts, we think of people and things. The same happens in real life. Seeing sees only visible object, and we take what we see for people or things which last. Persons are not real in the ultimate sense, no matter whether we see them on a screen or in the world around us. The world with people, living beings or things is real in conventional sense.

The Buddha taught that there is ultimate truth and conventional truth. We do not have to avoid thinking of conventional truth, of concepts of people and things; we could not lead our daily life without thinking of concepts and dealing with them. We have to pay attention to the people we meet in our social life, we could not give assistance to them without thinking of them in terms of concepts. When we develop generosity we need to think of the gift we wish to give and of the people to whom we are handing the gift. We could not develop kindness and compassion without thinking of people. However, we should know the difference between conventional truth and ultimate truth.

Right understanding can be developed so that it can be known when a paramattha dhamma, an ultimate reality, is the object of citta and when a concept. When we know that there is this person or that thing, we should realize that citta has arisen and knows at that moment a concept. The citta which thinks of a concept is a paramattha dhamma, the concept itself is not. In our daily life the object of citta is either a paramattha dhamma or a concept. The cittas which experience sense objects through the six doorways experience paramattha dhammas, but if satipaṭṭhāna is not developed it is not known that rūpas such as visible object or sound are paramattha dhammas. When satipaṭṭhāna is being developed a paramattha dhamma is the object of awareness, not a concept.

Only paramattha dhammas have the characteristics of impermanence, dukkha and anattā, non-self, which should be realized as they are, so that defilements can be eradicated. We may think of concepts with kusala citta or with akusala citta. The Buddha and the arahats also thought of concepts but they were not deluded about them, they had no defilements on account of them. If we cling to concepts and take them for things which really exist, which are permanent or self, we are deluding ourselves. Clinging to concepts of person or self leads to many other kinds of defilements, it leads to a great deal of sorrow.

When someone has lost a person who was dear to him, he seems to live with his memories of the person he loved, he lives with his dreams, with an illusion. However, also when a beloved person is still alive we live with our dreams; we take the person we believe we see, hear or touch for reality. Someone who is in love with another person is actually in love with a concept he conceives of that person, with an idealized image he has of that person. He may not have understanding of realities, of the different cittas which arise because of their approriate conditions. We may think of other people and have expectations about them which cannot come true; this leads to sorrow.

We have learnt about nāma and rūpa and about the conditions for their arising, but theoretical understanding is not enough. We should consider ultimate realities in daily life. We tend to forget that seeing is only a conditioned reality and that visible object is only a conditioned reality, and therefore we are easily carried away by sense impressions. It is beneficial to remember that seeing, hearing and the other sense-cognitions are vipākacittas, cittas which are results of kamma. They arise at their appropriate bases, vatthus, which are also produced by kamma. These bases have to arise before the sense-cognitions and they condition these by way of prenascent dependence-condition. Visible object and the other sense objects are rūpas which also have to arise before the sense-cognitions and which condition these by way of prenascent presence-condition. Each reality which arises does so because of a concurrence of different conditions which operate in a very intricate way. We should not try to pinpoint all the different conditions for the nāma and rūpa which appear. However, the study of different conditions helps us to understand that there isn't anybody who can control realities, that realities arise because of their own conditions. Nobody can cause the arising of seeing. There was also seeing in past lives and there will be seeing in next lives. Seeing only sees visible object. The object of seeing is always the same, visible object, but thinking thinks about what is seen in various ways: with ignorance or with right understanding. We ourselves and other people were different beings in past lives with different ways of thinking and we shall be different again in lives to come. We think with cittas conditioned by root-condition, hetu-paccaya; these cittas can have akusala hetus or sobhana hetus. On account of what is seen or heard there is happiness or sorrow, and we are ignorant of realities. In being mindful of one reality as it appears through one of the six doors, we shall know the difference between the moments of mindfulness of a reality and the moments of thinking of an image of a "whole", a person or a thing.

When there is right understanding of a reality as it appears one at a time, we do not expect other people to behave as we would like them to. Someone may insult us, but if we understand conditions for the phenomena which arise, we shall be less inclined to blame that person. When words of praise and blame are spoken to us, hearing the sound is vipākacitta, result produced by kusala kamma or akusala kamma. When we think about the meaning of the words which were spoken to us, defilements tend to arise.

As we have seen, even kusala can be a natural decisive support-condition, pakatūpanissaya-paccaya, for akusala[1]. When we perform good deeds we tend to cling to "our kusala", we want to be a "good person". While we study the conditions we learn that there are many factors which can condition akusala citta. Sense objects can condition akusala citta by way of object-condition, object predominance-condition or object decisive support-condition[2]. Akusala roots, hetus, condition akusala citta by way of root-condition, hetu-paccaya[3]. When akusala citta arises there is not only one type of citta but seven types since each javana-citta conditions the next one by way of repetition-condition, āsevana-paccaya[4]. When lobha-mūla-citta arises it can be the object of lobha-mūla-citta which arises in another process, because we enjoy having lobha, especially when it is accompanied by pleasant feeling. We accumulate clinging from life to life; the lobha which arises now is a natural decisive support-condition for lobha arising in the future. We may have regret about our attachment and then attachment is the object of dosa-mūla-citta with regret. Since we have accumulated such a great deal of defilements, our speech is produced more often by akusala citta than by kusala citta. We cling to speech and take it for self and "mine". However, as we have seen, it is citta which produces the rūpa which is speech intimation and it arises at the same time. There is no self who decides to speak and causes the arising of speech. Citta which produces rūpa conditions rūpa in many different ways: by conascence-condition[5], by dependence-condition[6], by nutriment-condition[7], by faculty-condition[8], by conascent dissociation-condition, by conascent presence-condition and non-disappearance-condition[9]. Whwn kusala citta or akusala citta produces rūpa, for example the rūpa which is speech intimation, the accompanying roots condition that rūpa by way of root-condition[10]. If citta is a predominant factor among the four factors which can be conascent predominance-condition[11], it conditions the rūpa it produces by way of conascent predominance-condition. The study of conditions makes it clearer to us that our life consists of fleeting phenomena which arise because of their own conditions and that there is no self who could control the events of our life.

There are many factors which condition akusala now and also in the future; by learning about these conditions we acquire more understanding of the danger of the

---

[1] See chapter 8.

[2] See chapters 2, 3 and 7.

[3] See chapter 1.

[4] See chapter 10.

[5] See chapter 5.

[6] See chapter 6.

[7] See chapter 12. Citta is one of the three mental nutriments and as such it can condition rūpa by way of nutriment-condition.

[8] See chapter 13. Citta is mind faculty, manindriya, and as such it can condition rūpa by way of faculty-condition.

[9] See for these last three conditions chapter 16.

[10] See chapter 1.

[11] See chapter 3. Chanda, desire-to-do, viriya, energy, citta and vimaṃsa, investigation of dhamma, are four factors which can be conascent predominance-condition. Only javana cittas accompanied by at least two roots can be predominance-condition.

accumulation of akusala. When we have understood that akusala leads to dukkha, we shall not forget the purpose of the study of Dhamma: the development of right understanding which leads to the eradication of clinging to the wrong view of self and of all defilements.

The study of conditions helps us to have more understanding of the factors which cause us to continue being in the cycle of birth and death. Because of ignorance and clinging life has to go on and on, until the cause of rebirth can be eliminated. There is no self who chose to be in the cycle of birth and death and there is no self who can eliminate the cause of rebirth. Everything occurs according to conditions, but this should not lead to discouragement. When we listen to the Dhamma and thoroughly consider it, we learn how to develop the right conditions leading to the end of dukkha.

In the "Kindred Sayings"(I, Sagāthā-vagga, V, Suttas of Sisters, paragraph 9), in the "Selā-sutta", we read that at Sāvatthī Māra addressed Sister Selā:

> "Who was it that made the human puppet's form?
> Where is the maker of the human doll?
> Whence, tell me, has the puppet come to be?
> Where will the puppet cease and pass away?"
>
> Selā answered:
>
> "Neither self-made the puppet is, nor yet
> By other wrought is this ill-plighted thing.
> By reason of a cause it came to be,
> By rupture of a cause it dies away.
> Like a certain seed sown in the field,
> Which, when it comes upon the taste of earth,
> And moisture likewise, by these two grows,
> So the five khandhas, the elements,
> And the six spheres of sense[12] even all these,
> By reason of a cause they came to be;
> By rupture of a cause they die away.
>
> Then Māra the evil one thought: Sister Selā knows me', and sad and sorrowful he vanished there and then."

---

12 Āyatanas.

Appendix 1

Sense-door process and mind-door process of cittas

When a sense object, which is rūpa, impinges on one of the sensedoors, it is experienced by several cittas arising in a sense-door process. Rūpa lasts as long as seventeen moments of citta and then it falls away. If rūpa arises at the moment of the "past bhavanga" and if the sense-door process of cittas runs its full course, there are, counting from the "past bhavanga", seventeen moments of citta. These seventeen moments of citta are as follows:

1. atīta-bhavanga (past bhavanga)
2. bhavanga calana (vibrating bhavanga)
3. bhavangupaccheda (arrest bhavanga, the last bhavanga arising before the object is experienced through the sense-door)
4. five-sense-door-adverting-consciousness (pañcadvārāvajjana-citta), which is a kiriyacitta
5. sense-cognition (dvi-pañcaviññāṇa, seeing-consciousness, etc.), which is vipākacitta
6. receiving-consciousness (sampaṭicchana-citta), which is vipākacitta
7. investigating-consciousness (santīraṇa-citta) which is vipākacitta
8. determining-consciousness (votthapana-citta) which is kiriyacitta
9. javana-citta ("impulsion", kusala citta or akusala citta in the case of non-arahats)
10. " "
11. " "
12. " "
13. " "
14. " "
15. " "
16. registering-consciousness (tadārammaṇa-citta) which is vipākacitta
17. registering-consciousness

A sense-door process does not always run its full course. When a rūpa impinges on one of the senses it may happen that more than three bhavanga-cittas pass before the sense-door adverting-consciousness arises, and then the process cannot run its full course, but it is interrupted earlier, since rūpa cannot last longer than seventeen moments of citta. The rūpa may have fallen away before the tadārammaṇa-citta is due to arise, and in that case the javana-cittas are the last cittas of that process. The process of cittas which experience rūpa may also end its course with the votthapana-citta, determining-consciousness, and then javana-cittas do not arise. Or it may happen that the "vibrating bhavanga", bhavanga calana, succeeds the past bhavanga, atīta-bhavanga, but that the arrest bhavanga, bhavangupaccheda (last bhavanga before the stream of bhavanga-cittas is arrested and a sense-door process begins), does not arise and then there cannot be any sense-door process. In that case there is a "futile course".

After a sense object has been experienced through a sense-door it is experienced through the mind-door, and then that object has just fallen away. Before the mind-door process begins there are bhavanga-cittas and the last two of these are specifically designated by a name. There are the following cittas:

- bhavanga calana (vibrating bhavanga)
- bhavangupaccheda (which is in this case the mind-door through which the cittas of the mind-door process will experience the object)
- mind-door-adverting-consciousness (mano-dvārāvajjana-citta) which is kiriyacitta
- 7 javana-cittas
- 2 tadārammaṇa-cittas (which may or may not arise).

After the mind-door process has been completed there are bhavanga-cittas again.

Appendix 2

Appendix to Ch 3, Conascent-Predominance-Condition.

The cittas which can be conascent-predominance-condition for the accompanying dammas, the cetasikas and mind-produced rūpa, are the cittas which perform the function of javana (impulsion) in the process of cittas and which are accompanied by at least two roots, hetus.

Altogether there are fifty-five types of citta which can perform the function of javana, but one of those is not accompanied by hetus, namely, the smile-producing consciousness of the arahat (hasituppāda citta). This is an ahetuka kiriyacitta which performs the function of javana[1], but since it is ahetuka, without roots, it cannot be predominance-condition. The two types of moha-mūla-citta, cittas rooted in ignorance, cannot be predominance-condition either since they have moha as their only root. Thus, out of the fiftyfive types of citta which can perform the function of javana, there are fiftytwo types of citta which can be predominance-condition. They are the following types:

- 8 lobha-mūla-cittas, cittas rooted in attachment
- 2 dosa-mūla-cittas, cittas rooted in aversion
- 8 mahā-kusala cittas
- 8 mahā-kiriyacittas
- 5 rūpāvacara kusala cittas
- 5 rūpāvacara kiriyacittas
- 4 arūpāvacara kusala cittas
- 4 arūpāvacara kiriyacittas
- 4 magga-cittas (path-consciousness, lokuttara kusala citta)
- 4 phala-cittas (fruition-consciousness, lokuttara vipākacitta)

Of the eight types of lobha-mūla-cittas, four are accompanied by wrong view, diṭṭhi, four are without wrong view, four are accompanied by pleasant feeling, four by indifferent feeling, four are unprompted, four are prompted (induced by someone else or by oneself). Of the two types of dosa-mūla-citta, one type is unprompted and one type is prompted.

Of the eight types of mahā-kusala cittas (kusala cittas of the sense-sphere) and of the eight types of mahā-kiriyacittas (kiriyacittas of the arahat which belong to the sense-sphere), there are four out of the eight types which are accompanied by paññā, and four which are unaccompanied by paññā, four which are accompanied by pleasant feeling and four which are accompanied by indifferent feeling, four which are unprompted, and four which are prompted.

[1] Arahats do not laugh aloud, because they have no accumulations for laughing, they only smile. When they smile it may be motivated by sobhana kiriyacitta (kiriyacitta accompanied by wholesome roots) or by ahetuka kiriyacitta which is called hasituppādacitta. This is the only kind of ahetuka kiriyacitta which can perform the function of javana.

The five types of rūpāvacāra cittas (kusala cittas and kiriyacittas of the arahat) are jhānacittas corresponding to the five stages of rūpa-jhāna, and the four types of arūpāvacara cittas (kusala cittas and kiriyacittas of the arahat) are jhānacittas corresponding to the four stages of arūpa-jhāna. All jhāna-cittas are accompanied by paññā. When jhāna is being developed there have to be one of the four predominant factors which condition the accompanying dhammas by way of predominance-condition.

There are four types of magga-cittas, lokuttara kusala cittas experiencing nibbāna, which correspond to the four stages of enlightenment. The four types of phala-cittas are lokuttara vipākacittas, the results of the magga-cittas. All lokuttara cittas are accompanied by paññā. The magga-citta is succeeded immediately by phala-citta within the process of cittas during which enlightenment is attained; the phala-citta is the only type of vipākacitta which performs the function of javana, and thus it can be predominance-condition. Lokuttara citta does not arise without conascent predominance-condition.

Thus, there are fiftytwo types of cittas performing the function of javana which can be conascent-predominance-condition for the accompanying dhammas: the cetasikas and mind-produced rūpa. The factors chanda and viriya, when they are predominance-condition, can arise only with these types of javana-cittas. As regards the factor vimaṃsa, investigation of Dhamma, this is paññā cetasika and, as we have seen, this does not arise with all sobhana cittas of the sense-sphere; all jhānacittas and all lokuttara cittas, however, are accompanied by paññā. Vimaṃsa can only be conascent-predominance-condition when it accompanies those javana-cittas which are associated with paññā.

Appendix 3

Appendix to Ch 10, Repetition-Condition.

The javana-cittas which can be repetition-condition are the following:

- 8 lobha-mūla-cittas, cittas rooted in attachment
- 2 dosa-mūla-cittas, cittas rooted in aversion
- 2 moha-mūla-cittas, cittas rooted in ignorance
- 8 mahā-kusala cittas
- 8 mahā-kiriyacittas
- 1 hasituppāda-citta (ahetuka kiriyacitta, smile producing citta of the arahat)
- 5 rūpāvacara kusala cittas
- 5 rūpāvacara kiriyacittas
- 4 arūpāvacara kusala cittas
- 4 arūpāvacara kiriyacittas

In the process when jhāna is attained there arise, after the mind-door adverting-consciousness (mano-dvārāvajjana-citta), first kāmāvacara cittas before jhāna-citta arises. These are, in the case of non-arahats, mahā-kusala cittas which experience the meditation subject through the mind-door. These cittas are:

- parikamma or preparatory consciousness
- upacāra, which means proximity or access
- anuloma, conformity or adaptation
- gotrabhū, change-of-lineage, which overcomes the sense sphere

Each one of these is repetition-condition for the next one and the last mahā-kusala citta in that process, the gotrabhū, conditions the jhāna-citta by way of repetition-condition.

In the process during which enlightenment is attained, there are, after the mano-dvārāvajjana-citta, three mahā-kusala cittas accompanied by paññā which clearly see the reality appearing at that moment as impermanent, dukkha or anattā. These mahā-kusala cittas are:

- parikamma, preparatory-consciousness
- upacāra, proximity or access
- anuloma, conformity or adaptation
- Anuloma is succeeded by gotrabhū or change-of-lineage, the last kāmāvacara kusala citta before lokuttara cittas arise. The change-of-lineage experiences nibbāna.

Each of these mahā-kusala cittas is repetition-condition for the next one. The last mahā-kusala-citta, the "change-of lineage", arising before the magga-citta, conditions the magga-citta by way of repetition-condition but the magga-citta itself is not repetition-condition for the phala-citta. The phala-citta, which is vipākacitta, is not repetition-condition either.

Thus, there are 29 kāmāvacara cittas, cittas of the sense-sphere, and 18 jhānacittas which can be repetition-condition. The lokuttara kusala cittas, magga-cittas, and the lokuttara vipākacittas, phala-cittas, are excluded.

Glossary

abhidhamma	the higher teachings of Buddhism, teachings on ultimate realities
adhipati-paccaya	predominance condition
adosa	non aversion
āhāra-paccaya	nutriment-condition
ahetukacittas	not accompanied by "beautiful roots" or unwholesome roots
ājīva-duccarita	virati abstinence from wrong livelihood
ākāsānañcāyatana	sphere of boundless space, the meditation subject of the first immaterial jhānacitta
akiriya-diṭṭhi	The view that there is no such thing as kamma
akusala citta	unwholesome consciousness
akusala kamma	bad deed
akusala	unwholesome, unskilful
alobha	non-attachment, generosity
amoha	wisdom or understanding
anāgāmī	non-returner, person who has reached the third stage of enlightenment, he has no aversion (dosa)
anantara-paccaya	proximity-condition
anantarika kamma	heinous crimes
anattā	not self
anicca	impermanence.
aññamañña-paccaya	mutuality-condition
aññindriya	The faculty of final knowledge , which arises at the moment of the phala-citta, fruition-consciousness, of the sotāpanna, and also accompanies the magga-citta and the phala-citta of the sakadāgāmī and of the anāgāmī and the magga-citta of the arahat
apo-dhātu	element of water or cohesion
arahat	noble person who has attained the fourth and last stage of enlightenment
ārammaṇa	object which is known by consciousness.
ariyan	noble person who has attained enlightenment
āsevana-paccaya	repetition-condition
atthi-paccaya	presence-condition
avigata-paccaya	non-disappearance-condition
balas	powers, strengths
bhaṅgakhaṇa	dissolution moment of citta

bhavangupaccheda	arrest bhavanga, last bhavanga-citta before a process of cittas starts
bhikkhu	monk
bhikkhuṅnī	nun
bhūmi	existence or plane of citta
bodhisatta	being destined to become a Buddha
Brahma	heavenly being born in the Brahma world, as a result of the attainment of jhāna
Buddha	fully enlightened person who has discovered the truth all by himself, without the aid of a teacher
Buddhaghosa	the greatest of Commentators on the Tipiṭaka, author of the Visuddhimagga in 5 A.D.
cakkhu	eye
cakkhu-dhātu	eye element
cetanā	volition
chanda	"wish to do"
citta	consciousness, the reality which knows or cognizes an object
cutiicitta	dying-consciousness
dāna	generosity, giving
diṭṭhi	wrong view, distorted view of realities
domanassa	unpleasant feeling
dosa	aversion or ill will
gotrabhū	change of lineage, the last citta of the sense-sphere before jhāna, absorption, is attained, or enlightenment is attained
hadaya-vatthu	heart-base, rūpa which is the plane of origin of the cittas other than the sense-cognitions.
hasituppāda-citta	smile-producing-consciousness of an arahat
hetu	root, which conditions citta to be"beautiful" or unwholesome
hiri	moral shame
iddhipādas	four"Roads to Success"
indriya	faculty. Some are rūpas such as the sense organs, some are nāmas such as feeling. Five 'spiritual faculties' are wholesome faculties which should be cultivated, namely: confidence, energy, awareness, concentration and wisdom.
indriya-paccaya	faculty-condition
issā	envy
jāti	birth, nature, class (of cittas)
javana	impulsion, running through the object
javana-citta	cittas which 'run through the object', kusala citta or akusala citta in the case of non-arahats

jhāna	absorption which can be attained through the development of calm
jhāna-paccaya	jhāna-condition
jivhā-viññāṇa	tasting-consciousness
jīvitindriya	life-faculty or vitality
kāma	sensual enjoyment or the five sense objects.
kāmāvacara cittas	cittas of the sense sphere
kamma	intention or volition; deed motivated by volition.
kamma patha	course of action performed through body, speech or mind which can be wholesome or unwholesome
kamma-paccaya	kamma-condition
kāya	body. It can also stand for the 'mental body', the cetasikas
khandhas	aggregates of conditioned realities classified as five groups: physical phenomena, feelings, perception or remembrance, activities or formations (cetasikas other than feeling or perception), consciousness.
kiriyacitta	inoperative citta, neither cause nor result
kukkucca	regret or worry
kusala citta	wholesome consciousness
kusala kamma	good deed
lakkhaṇa	characteristic, specific or generic attribute
lobha	attachment, greed
lobha-mūla-citta	consciousness rooted in attachment
lokiya citta	citta which is mundane, not experiencing nibbāna
lokuttara citta	supramundane citta which experiences nibbāna
magga	path (eightfold Path)
magga-citta	path-consciousness, supramundane citta which experiences nibbāna and eradicates defilements
magga-paccaya	path-condition
manasikāra	attention
mano	mind, citta, consciousness
māra	"the evil one"-all that leads to dukkha
mettā	loving kindness
micchā-diṭṭhi	wrong view
middha	torpor or languor
moha	ignorance
moha-mūla-cittas	cittas rooted in ignorance
nāmakkhandha	group of all mental phenomena

nāma	mental phenomena,including those which are conditioned and also the unconditioned nāma which is nibbāna
natthi-paccaya	absence-condition
nibbāna	unconditioned reality, the reality which does not arise and fall away. The destruction of lust, hatred and delusion. The deathless. The end of suffering
nissaya-paccaya	dependence-condition
ojā	the rūpa which is nutrition
paccayas	conditions
pacchājāta-paccaya	postnascence-condition
paṭiccasammuppada	'Dependent Origination', the conditional origination of phenomena
paṭigha	aversion or ill will
Paṭṭhāna	Conditional Relations, one of the seven books of the Abhidhamma
Pāli	the language of the Buddhist teachings
paññā	wisdom or understanding
paññatti	concepts, conventional terms
paramattha dhamma	truth in the absolute sense: mental and physical phenomena, each with their own characteristic.
pasāda-rūpas	rūpas which are capable of receiving sense-objects such as visible object, sound, taste, etc.
phala-citta	fruition-consciousness experiencing nibbāna. It is result of magga-citta, path-consciousness.
phassa	contact
pīti	joy, rapture, enthusiasm
purejāta-paccaya	prenascence-condition
puthujjana	"worldling", a person who has not attained enlightenment
rūpa	physical phenomena, realities which do not experience anything
rūpāvacaracittas	rūpa-jhānacittas, consciosness of the fine-material sphere
saddhā	confidence
sahajāta-paccaya	conascence-condition
sakadāgāmī	once-returner, a noble person who has attained the second stage of enlightenment
samādhi	concentration or one-pointedness, ekaggatā cetasika
samanantara-paccaya	contiguity-condition
samatha	the development of calm
sampayutta	associated with
sampayutta-paccaya	association-condition

saññā	memory, remembrance or "perception"
saṅkhārakkhandha	all cetasikas (mental factors) except feeling and memory.
saṅkhāra dhamma	conditioned realities
Sāriputta	The chief disciple of the Buddha
sasaṅkhārika	prompted, induced, instigated, either by oneself or someone else
sati	awareness, non-forgetfulness, awareness of reality by direct experience
satipaṭṭhāna	applicatioms of mindfulness. It can mean the cetasika sati which is aware of realities or the objects of mindfulness which are classified as four applications of mindfulness: Body, Feeling Citta, Dhamma. Or it can mean the development of direct understanding of realities through awareness.
satipaṭṭhāna sutta	Middle Length Sayings 1, number 10, also Dīgha Nikāya, Dialogues 11, no. 22
sīla	morality in action or speech, virtue
sobhana (citta and cetasika)	beautiful, accompanied by beautiful roots
somanassa	happy feeling
sotāpanna	person who has attained the first stage of enlightenment, and who has eradicated wrong view of realities
sukha	happy, pleasant
sutta	part of the scriptures containing dialogues at different places on different occasions
Tathāgata	literally "thus gone", epithet of the Buddha
tejo-dhātu	element of fire or heat
Theravāda Buddhism	'Doctrine of the Elders', the oldest tradition of Buddhism
Tipiṭaka	the teachings of the Buddha
uddhacca	restlessness
upacāra	access or proximatory consciousness, the second javana-citta in the process in which absorption or enlightenment is attained
upanissaya-paccaya	decisive support-condition
upekkhā	indifferent feeling. It can stand for evenmindedness or equanimity and then it is not feeling
vacī-duccarita virati	abstinence from wrong speech
vacī viññatti	the rūpa which is speech intimation

vāsanā	disagreeable habits accumulated in the past that can only be eradicated by a Buddha. Even arahats who have eradicated all defilements may still have a way of speech or action that is not agreeable to others
vatthu	base, physical base of citta
vāyo-dhātu	element of wind or motion
vedanā	feeling
vedanākkhandha	group of all feelings
Vibhaṅga	"Book of Analysis", one of the seven books of the Abhidhamma
vibhava-taṇhā	craving for non-existence
vicāra	sustained thinking or discursive thinking
vicikicchā	doubt
vigata-paccaya	disappearance-condition
vihiṁsā-vitakka	thought of harming
vinaya	Book of Discipline for the monks
viññāṇa	consciousness, citta
viññāṇa-dhātu	element of consciousness, comprising all cittas.
viññāṇakkhandha	all cittas (consciousness)
vipāka-paccaya	vipāka-condition
vipākacitta	citta which is the result of a wholesome deed (kusala kamma) or an unwholesome deed (akusala kamma). It can arise as rebirth-consciousness, or during life as the experience of pleasant or unpleasant objects through the senses, such as seeing, hearing, etc.
vipassanā	wisdom which sees realities as they are
vippayutta	dissociated from
vippayutta-paccaya	dissociation-condition
viriya	energy
visaṅkāra dhamma	unconditioned dhamma (reality)
Visuddhimagga	an encyclopaedia of the Buddha's teaching, written by Buddhaghosa in the fifth century A.D.
vitakka	applied thinking

Books

Books written by Nina van Gorkom

- *The Buddha's Path* An Introduction to the doctrine of Theravada Buddhism for those who have no previous knowledge. The four noble Truths - suffering - the origin of suffering - the cessation of suffering - and the way leading to the end of suffering - are explained as a philosophy and a practical guide which can be followed in today's world.
- *Buddhism in Daily Life* A general introduction to the main ideas of Theravada Buddhism.The purpose of this book is to help the reader gain insight into the Buddhist scriptures and the way in which the teachings can be used to benefit both ourselves and others in everyday life.
- *Abhidhamma in Daily Life* is an exposition of absolute realities in detail. Abhidhamma means higher doctrine and the book's purpose is to encourage the right application of Buddhism in order to eradicate wrong view and eventually all defilements.
- *The World in the Buddhist Sense* The purpose of this book is to show that the Buddha's Path to true understanding has to be developed in daily life.
- *Cetasikas* Cetasika means 'belonging to the mind'. It is a mental factor which accompanies consciousness (citta) and experiences an object. There are 52 cetasikas. This book gives an outline of each of these 52 cetasikas and shows the relationship they have with each other.
- *The Buddhist Teaching on Physical Phenomena* A general introduction to physical phenomena and the way they are related to each other and to mental phenomena. The purpose of this book is to show that the study of both mental phenomena and physical phenomena is indispensable for the development of the eightfold Path.

Books translated by Nina van Gorkom

- *Metta: Loving kindness in Buddhism* by Sujin Boriharnwanaket. An introduction to the basic Buddhist teachings of metta, loving kindness, and its practical application in todays world.
- *Taking Refuge in Buddhism* by Sujin Boriharnwanaket. Taking Refuge in Buddhism is an introduction to the development of insight meditation.
- *A Survey of Paramattha Dhammas* by Sujin Boriharnwanaket. A Survey of Paramattha Dhammas is a guide to the development of the Buddha's path of wisdom, covering all aspects of human life and human behaviour, good and bad. This study explains that right understanding is indispensable for mental development, the development of calm as well as the development of insight.
- *The Perfections Leading to Enlightenment* by Sujin Boriharnwanaket. The Perfections is a study of the ten good qualities: generosity, morality, renunci-

ation, wisdom, energy, patience, truthfulness, determination, loving-kindness, and equanimity.

These and other articles can be seen at www.zolag.co.uk or www.scribd.com (search for zolag).

www.ingramcontent.com/pod-product-compliance
Lightning Source LLC
Chambersburg PA
CBHW081151090426
42736CB00017B/3278
* 9 7 8 1 8 9 7 6 3 3 2 6 7 *